Police

What You Don't Know

Attention Authors

'We Convert Fighters into Writers'. That has been the motto of Manas Publications, since more than four decades. Our message to the world is that India can win the battle, not only by the bullet but also by the pen. There is no dearth of intellectuals in our country, but their knowledge is confined to them only. No sincere effort has, so far, been made by any other publisher to channelise their knowledge in national interest. That is why the talent of a large number of intellectuals, remains latent. An author transforms his knowledge, into a manuscript, and it is our job to spread his/her knowledge by converting it into a beautiful book.

For over four decades, Manas has been motivating the intellectuals by publishing their manuscripts and would like to publish your manuscript too. If you or your colleagues have any manuscript, ready for publication or are working on it, kindly contact us with detailed synopsis and the list of contents. We would transform your work, into a valuable publication. If you wish, we can also suggest you, the suitable subjects for writing books, related to your area of expertise. Manas is known for its publishing quality and commitments. We take utmost care in production and give wide publicity to the book, as well as its author, through our national and international distribution network.

Police
What You Don't Know

Dr DV Guruprasad, IPS
(Former DGP – Karnataka)

Manas Publications
(We Convert Fighters into Writers)
New Delhi-110002 (INDIA)

MANAS PUBLICATIONS
(We Convert Fighters into Writers)

(Publishers, Distributors, Importers & Exporters)
4402/5-A, Ansari Road (Opp. HDFC Bank)
Darya Ganj, New Delhi-110 002 (India)
Off. 23260783, 23265523, Res. 23842660
Fax: 011-23272766
E-mail: manaspublications@gmail.com
manaspub6@gmail.com
Website: www.manaspublications.in

ISBN 978-81-7049-532-1
₹ 595/-

Designed at Innovative Processors

Printed in India at
R.K. Print Service, Delhi and
Published by Mrs Suman Lata for
Manas Publications, 4402/5-A, Ansari Road (Opp. HDFC Bank),
Darya Ganj, New Delhi-110 002 (INDIA)

Contents

Introduction 9

1. Excellent Pranks of Chinese Puppy 13
2. Reversal of Roles 16
3. An Ecstasy with Police Wireless 19
4. Lady Cop in 'Undress': A Laughing Stock 22
5. Outwitting the Boss 25
6. With Balaji's Blessing 28
7. Over a (Hot) Cup of Tea 31
8. Car Without a Steering Wheel 34
9. Small Savings in England 37
10. Cattle Station 40
11. The King's Gift 43
12. Gratitude is Still Alive 45

13. Occupational Hazard 48
14. Bitten by Publicity 51
15. Vanishing Trick 54
16. Minister's Footwear 57
17. Royal Repast Festivity 60
18. Prestige Regained 63
19. Recovery Police Style 65
20. Swalpa Adjust Maadi 68
21. Like Poles Repel 72
22. Sparrows in a Distant Land 75
23. Modelling Blues 77
24. Staying Young: A Day Dreaming 79
25. Watching a Tragic Play 81
26. Dogged Perseverance: A Positive Conversion of Arrogance 83
27. Be an Assamese 86
28. Last Ride Together 88
29. (Imaginary) Lunch with Musharraf 91
30. An 'Indian' Wedding 94
31. Unholy Water 97
32. Rome Wasn't Built in a Day 99
33. Mayor's Dinner 102
34. Nature's Call 105
35. My Day at the Races 108
36. Exchange Mela: Buy New, Give Old 111
37. Bitter Dharwad Pedas 114
38. Senior Bureaucrat and the Common People's Party 117
39. The Day I Dyed 120
40. Zest For Life 123
41. My Tryst with Customs Officials 126
42. Friday, the Thirteenth: Impact of Ritual Restriction 129
43. How Hapless are Dogs in India 132
44. Nourishing the Soul 135
45. Vagaries of Vaccination 138

46. Grandpa's Joy: An Attachment at Rise 141
47. The Case of the Missing Footwear 144
48. Brimming with Pride 147
49. The Joy of HMT Watch 150
50. Mornings, a City's Mirror 153
51. My Special GPS 156
52. Age Cannot Wither Lady Countenance 158
53. Fascinating Chanakyapuri 161
54. Nectar-Drops of Human Kindness 164
55. Are You Alive, Sir? 167
56. Belgian Chocolates 169

Index 173

Introduction

When I was a student of literature, I had read a story of a dhobi and a policeman. A dhobi would be walking along a road taking his donkey to the tank for washing clothes. A VIP would be scheduled to travel on that road. Seeing the dhobi with his donkey, a Police Officer on guard of VIP thinks that it would hamper the VIP movement. He calls a constable standing nearby shouts at him for allowing the dhobi and his donkey to walk along the VIP route. The chastised constable summons the dhobi and thrashes him hard and harsh with *lathi*. The Dhobi is shocked and humiliated but he cannot vent his ire on the cop. He therefore, takes a stick and beats his donkey black and blue. Excellent was that revenge.

When I joined the Police Department as an IPS officer, I kept glued this story to my heart. During the thirty six years service with department, I came across a number of incidents which are similar to the story of police and the washer man. The incidents that I came to experience are not only funny and amusing but also show the distinct sub-culture in which the police functions or in other words redtapism. Many incidents that I have seen can happen only in the police environment and nowhere else. The hierarchical setup lays emphasis on discipline, desire to please one's bosses and display of power over a common man. These traits are common in police sub-culture.

I started writing about these incidents. Since in those days, there were no blocade, I sent them to newspapers for publication at "middle" in the editorial page. *Deccan Herald,* a prominent English newspaper emanating from Bangalore published my first "middle" sometime in the early 90s. Subsequently, I contributed "middles" to the newspapers regularly.

A collection of twenty five "middles" was published in 2007 as "Funny side of Police life". This collection received encouraging reviews and many readers wanted me to write more which I did with religious regularity.

After I retired from service in 2011, I concentrated more on incidents whose subject was not necessarily police. Whatever I observed as a retired officer, whatever I experienced during my regular stints in foreign countries all that became subject of my "middles" . However, because of my training, I saw things only through the eyes of a cop.

After publication of more than fifty anecdotes in newspapers, my friends desired that I should publish a second collection. The book you are now reading is its result. This book contains more than fifty episodes and most of them were published in *Deccan Herald*. Of course, all the stories that found a place in the first collection "Funny side of police life" find a place here too.

I feel that these incidents are a mirror of police life in India, especially in South India, during the last four decades. I hope readers will find the collection very interesting, enjoyable and also inspiring to bring in some exemplary reforms in temperament of bureaucrats.

I am thankful to Manas Publications, New Delhi for coming forward to publish this book. In fact, this is the second work of mine being published by Manas Publications.

Dr. D.V. Guruprasad

1

Excellent Pranks of Chinese Puppy

It was a chilly December night in Delhi when my visitor said that he had a gift for me. Slowly, he unbuttoned his jacket and took out a tiny thing with a flourish and placed it on the table. The visitor said that it was a pedigreed Lhasa apso pup, a female. "She is only three weeks old and our boss wants you to christen her with a name beginning with the letter 's'. So saying, he left the pup in my hands and left.

"Papa, she's so pinky, pinky and has no hair, is she really an Apso?" Queried my daughter, while my son asked, "Dad! is she Pomeranian or a Lhasa?" My wife said "We will call her Sweety". While my son suggested the name Susan, my daughter who is a tennis fan, wanted us to call the dog Steffi. I said, "Since she is Tibetan dog and since Tibet is in China, we will give her a Chinese name which will be **Suzy Wong**". All the three agreed to this suggestion, took the pup inside and made her comfortable by putting her in an old shoe box lined with newspapers.

When Govindasamy, our Police orderly, came home for duty the next morning, the kids introduced him to the new family member. Govindasamy said that he would call the dog by a name he is familiar with – Susheela! Soon 'Suzy' got accustomed to our family and by her puppy pranks, become the most talked about pup in the neighbourhood.

The following week, all of us had to go on a two-day trip to Chandigarh and the kids wanted to take Suzy along. With great difficulty, I could convince them that Suzy is too small and needs constant care, which we can't give during our trip. We then asked Govindasamy to sleep in our house and look after "Susheela" till we returned.

The kids reluctantly agreed to leave Suzy at home. Every moment during our tour, they would ask about Suzy and wanted to phone home and check about her welfare. The trip soon ended. When we returned home, before Govindasamy could open the door fully, the kids barged into look for Suzie. As we entered, Govindasamy suddenly prostrated before me, and holding my feet firmly, began sobbing. "Sir, please forgive me. At five this evening I went out to buy *beedies* keeping "Susheela" in her box and locking the main door. I returned after ten minutes and found "Susheela" missing. I searched everywhere in the house but could not find her. In fact, the balcony door was open and probably the pup must have fallen down. Sir, till you forgive me I will not leave your feet".

Hearing this, my kids started sobbing too and my wife started humiliating Govindasamy for his callousness and wanted me to suspend him forthwith. I philosophized stating, "Look! one day Suzy had to die. It's good that the pup died so early before we could get attached to her even more. Who can change fate?" Before I could say anything further, my wife and kids stormed away. I shouted at Govindasamy, warned him to be careful and asked him to get out.

After reading the mail, I went to my bedroom to find my sulking wife, already covering her head with the *razai*. I slowly undressed, opened my wardrobe, and as I jerked out my lungi from the bottommost part of the wardrobe, I felt some warm object. Startled, I switched on the light to see '"Susheela" opening her small eyes and prancing about! When Govindasamy had gone out, Suzy had probably entered the open wardrobe, and finding warmth in the cold weather, had parked herself there.

2

Reversal of Roles

When I was promoted as Superintendent of Police of a district, I had just got married. My wife who was too scared to stay alone in the sprawling SP's bungalow, would accompany me on most of my tours. Once, I was to inspect a police station situated in a place famous for its Shiva temple, and I took my wife along. On arrival, my wife enquired about the temple with the Station House Officer. Quickly realizing that the visit would substantially cut the inspection time, the officer raved about the temple's historical significance and said that Lord Shiva would grant all boons to newly married couples who visit the temple especially on a Monday, which happened to be the next day! My wife quickly swallowed the bait and insisted on the temple visit, the very next morning.

The next morning, after the Parade, I had my bath and we both went to the temple accompanied by the Sub-Inspector. Since the Sub Inspector had ensured that we were the only ones present in the premises, we had an excellent *darshan*. After the *aarathi* the priest brought us hot *pongal* and curd rice as *prasadam*. Fully satisfied, my wife gave a handsome amount to the priest, touched his feet and asked me to do likewise.

The moment I bent down, the priest said, "Sir, you are the SP of this district. How can I allow you to touch my feet, please sir! It is okay, you need not prostrate". I looked up and found the face to be familiar and said, "It is okay *pujariji*. In the presence of the Lord, none of us is big. It is customary for us to prostrate, please allow me to do this".

My wife nodded in agreement but the Sub Inspector said, "Madam, *saab* is the SP of this district and there is no need for him to do this. Please come, we'll go to the Inspection Bungalow, the breakfast is getting cold". The lady would not agree and told him that if we do not take the blessings of the priest, our entire visit would be a waste.

As I bent down to touch his feet again, the priest started moving backwards as though a snake was about to bite him! The Sub-Inspector also urged me to come away. My wife then asked the priest not to embarrass us but to go ahead with the ritual. The priest then started shivering and said, "Madam, how can *saab* touch my feet. I would be committing a grave sin if I allowed it."

Before we could find how it would be a sin, the priest suddenly fell at my feet and said, "Sir! please forgive me. I am not the priest of this temple - my cousin is. On coming to know of your visit, the Station House Officer informed him to be ready for your *puja*. But since he had to go to the neighboring village for some urgent ritual, the Sub-Inspector asked me to officiate as the priest". "What if you aren't the real priest? We are satisfied by your performance," said my wife. Shivering, the *pujari* firmly held my feet and would not let go.

To our quizzical looks, the Sub-Inspector said, "Madam, since I had told you that Monday is auspicious to perform *pujas* here, I could not muster the courage to tell you that the priest is not available. Besides, I thought that *saab* would get angry and may pick out many faults during his inspection of the Police Station and place me under suspension. Hence, I directed my constable Ramanna to officiate as the priest in place of his cousin, the real priest. How can the SP touch the feet of his constable, madam?"

It was my turn to tell my wife that only policemen can be the men for all reasons.

3

An Ecstasy with Police Wireless

I had just started my practical training as an IPS officer in a north Karnataka district. Within a week of my reporting for duty, the Director General of Police (DGP) of the State intended to inspect the district and as was customary then, the Superintendent of Police (SP) with other officials went to the district border to receive the DGP. As we were waiting for the DGP's convoy, I heard a message over the wireless announcing "DGP passed away Ramapura". Startled, I went to the SP who was standing at the other side of the road and said that a serious tragedy had occurred. The SP who had also overheard the message had a hearty laugh and told me not to worry as the DGP had crossed Ramapura and the wireless operator who knows little English has only mentioned about the passage of the convoy. The SP said "Look, these wireless chaps have killed me so many times that nowadays if I have to convey on wireless that my vehicle has passed Kudligi, I too say that SP passed way Kudligi!"

A few weeks later, I was posted to a police station to learn the station work. As I was about to go for lunch, I heard a radio message that in five minutes Sugar Peter would be visiting that police station. I assumed that Sugar Peter must be a dignitary from Europe or must be someone who is a dealer of sugar. While I was wondering as to why he should come to the station, the car of the SP screeched to halt in front of the police station and as the SP walked in, I innocently told him that Mr.Sugar Peter is visiting the station and I am waiting for him. The SP had a big laugh and said that he himself is Sugar Peter as in police wireless terminology, 'S' stands for Sugar and 'P' for Peter! I had to politely tell him that in the police Academy, we would call SP as "Seara Pappa" and hence, my confusion.

When I was working in my first Sub-Division as an Asst. Superintendent of Police, my jeep driver Basanna also doubled as the radio operator. On the first day of my office, as I sat in the jeep to go to a police station, Basanna took the wireless and announced "Mike Two leaving for Rural Police Station". The constable manning the control room recognized Basanna's voice immediately and said "What Basanna, why was your wife quarreling with you this morning? Is everything alright?" Basanna became red in the face and reprimanded him by saying "Look Pandu! our new ASP has taken charge and is sitting in my jeep. I warn you not to use police wireless for private conversation."

As an ASP, once I went to the railway station to receive a VIP. The Station Master told me that the train would arrive in about half an hour but there was no sign of the VIP. I asked the Police Control Room to ascertain the location of the VIP and I was told that the gentleman is having tea in a Circuit House - 30 kms away. I kept on waiting and as soon the train steamed in, worried that the VIP would miss the train, I asked the wireless operator to find out where the VIP is. The following conversation ensued between the control room and the VIP's escort vehicle: "Where is your location, escort? The train has already arrived". "Control, we are still at the circuit house. Minister is having tea". "Why does your VIP take so long to have his tea, can you not go to his room and hurry him up?"

"Control, how can I do that? The *saab* has gone to the lavatory. Nobody here has the guts to call him out from there. What can we do?"

The above conversation broadcast over the wireless set of my jeep, made the people around laugh so loudly, I quietly left the scene. Needless to say, the VIP missed his train. From that day onwards, whenever I felt bored, I would listen to the wireless broadcasts and thoroughly enjoy myself.

4

Lady Cop in 'Undress': A Laughing Stock

Returning home one night, riding a borrowed bicycle while in college , I was 'caught' by a police constable for riding 'a bike without light'. Keen on returning the bike to its owner, I pleaded with the constable to excuse me and let me go. When it didn't work, I cajoled him and even offered him a tip but he was very firm and said "This is only a *pity case*, you can come to the court tomorrow and get your bicycle back."

I had then thought that the magistrate would take pity on me and would release the bike. Nothing of that sort happened. In the court, when I was ordered to pay a 'royal' fine of two rupees, I asked the magistrate innocently why I was being fined since it is a pity case. He started laughing and said, "No dear sir, this is not pity case, but a petty case!"

While I knew that police use their own language (which is usually abusive), only after I joined the department did I learn that the police use a type of language which is only understood by them. Though in the Police Training College, one gets familiar with police terminology, the terms differ from state to state. For example, in Haryana an SP is called a '*Kaptaan saab*', whereas in Calcutta a sub-inspector is called 'OC'. In Karnataka, if you call a Station House Officer an 'OC' you are most likely to end up losing your teeth as it is a slang for getting things for free. In Uttar Pradesh, while performing drill, if you tell a constable that you are confined to lines, the constable may go home. If you tell the same to a PC in Bangalore, he will probably join the drill platoon. Hence, during the first year of service in the States, we tend to get confused over certain phrases of use leading to amusing situations.

When we finished our training and came to Bangalore, we were to call on the senior officers of the state. The Liaison Officer who was attached to us said, "Tomorrow morning at 9 am sharp, come to the Chief Office in First dress." Those of us who didn't understand the terms 'first dress', and 'Chief Office' got clarification that they mean the ceremonial tunic and the DGPs office respectively. Before we got this clarification, our Colleague Vohra had left us to meet a friend.

The next day, when we all assembled at the office of the DGP, Vohra was not to be seen at all. When we went back to our mess, we learnt that Vohra had thought Vidhana Soudha (the building of the State Secretariat) to be the chief office and had gone there at 9 am sharp wearing his 'best dress'. He said having gone there, he called on the Home Secretary who ticked him off for coming without an appointment and that too wearing a civilian dress and not the khaki uniform.

Since Police officers do not wear their uniform all the time, the civilian clothes they wear is called different names in different places. Some call it 'civvies', some 'civilian dress' and in Karnataka it is called *'mufty'*. Once, I had gone to Kanyakumari along with my wife. My batch mate who was the SP there, had detailed a lady police officer to take us round the temples and other sight-seeing places. The lady cop who met us in the circuit house in the evening told us that we could visit the temple at early hours of the morning and that she would ensure a satisfactory visit. As she was leaving our room, she stood to attention and giving a smart salute asked me, "Sir, is it okay if I come in undress?" I said that I don't mind at all and in fact, prefer her to be in undress. She went away.

Soon afterwards, when we were alone in the room, my wife, started shouting at me saying, "You are such a senior police officer, and don't you have any sense of shame? In front of your wife, you are asking that female cop to come in undress tomorrow?!"

It took me more than an hour to convince her that in the State of Tamil Nadu which we were visiting, the police term 'undress' actually means 'civilian' dress!

5

Outwitting the Boss

"Hello Guru! this is Raghavan speaking. Next week our IGP is inspecting your police stations. Get started right away," said my SP over the phone. "Sir! this is my first charge as Assistant SP. I have reported for duty only ten days ago and how can I face the IGP's inspection so soon?" I asked with trepidition. "Look, his tour programme is already issued and he is known not to change his schedule. You better visit all the Police Stations you supervise, get the records updated and see that the buildings get a face-lift", was my SP's casual reply.

Soon I got in touch with the Inspectors of Town and Rural Police stations and informed them about the visit. Within the next three days, both the stations were given a face-lift.

The D-Day came. At the Rural Police Station, the inspection went off smoothly and before writing his remarks, the IG desired to test the men on their knowledge of drill. The twenty odd men were lined up in the parade ground and were put through arms drill. Soon the IG who seemed satisfied about the performance, called the Inspector and pointing at a constable, asked him to tell the PC's name. The Inspector said: "Sir he is PC NO.222 Ramakrishna." The IG then asked: "Where does this PC live and how many children does he have?" The Inspector said that he didn't know these details.

The IG suddenly became angry and shouting at the inspector said: "What kind of a leader are you? You don't even know the family particulars of one of the thirty men you command. I am very unhappy. You will be placed under suspension". Immediately, thereafter the IG asked to be taken to the Town Police Station. The sudden turn of events totally unnerved me and the cotton shirt under my ceremonial tunic had become totally wet. My SP squeezed my hand and asked me to take it in my stride.

The IG's cavalcade next landed at the Town Police Station nearby. The boss who was very angry started pointing out various small mistakes and did not accept the tea and biscuits placed before him. But somehow the inspection of records ended well. The IG then got up and went to the parade ground. I became very nervous since the Town Police Station had more than sixty men and the Inspector, being a newcomer, didn't know the names of even ten of his men!

After the ceremonial parade, the IG pointed his finger at one of the constables and asked the Inspector about details of the constable. The Inspector came to attention and in a very confident manner said: "Sir, he is Panduranga from Bellary. He has three kids -two boys and a girl. One of his sons is doing BE. His first daughter is in 12th standard and the last one is in 9th standard. He is staying in our police lines." The IG was thoroughly impressed by this prompt reply and turning to us said: "We should have more inspectors like this one." He then shook hands with me, and saying that he is satisfied, went away with the SP.

Heaving a sigh of relief, I took off my jacket, and went into the Inspector's room and called for a cup of tea. When I saw the constable who was pointed out by the IG, I called him saying, "Panduranga, come here." The PC was not amused. He said: "Sir, my name is Christopher. I live in a room nearby and I don't have children as I am not yet married!". Seeing the quizzical look on my face, the PC added: "Sir, we knew what happened in the Rural PS. Our inspector said that since he didn't want all of us to get a bad name, we should nod our head to whatever he said before the IG. I only obeyed him."

6

With Balaji's Blessing

Sitting in my office as Commandant of a Central Police Unit in South India, I received information that our IG would inspect my unit the very next week. Being new to that office, I was perturbed. The mercurial temper of our chief was well known; not satisfied with the work of a Commandant in Kerala, the Chief had transferred him to Mizoram!

As I was sitting forlorn, my Deputy Commandant Sharma breezed in and said, "Why are you so much worried, Sir? I have worked with our Chief earlier. You leave the matters to me." I agreed.

During the next three days, Sharmaji got the office premises whitewashed, got the registers updated, made the constables polish all the brass articles making the unit look spic-and-spam.

I received the IG and his wife on arrival. After he settled down at the Guest House, Sharmaji came in and smartly saluted the IG. "Hello Sharmaji! how are you? How is your family? How are things at your unit?" enquired the IG. "Sir, with Lord Balaji's and your blessings, everything is fine. Sir, by the way, I had been to the temple to pray for the success of our inspection. I told the priest about your visit. He said that since you are Balaji's ardent devotee, you should visit the temple with Madam tomorrow morning itself, since it is *Shravan* Saturday," said Sharma.

Sharmaji, how can I visit the temple in the morning? Have I not fixed the inspection of your unit at 9 am?" asked the IG. "Sir, the priest said that since Madam is with you, you should start your day with the *darshan* of Lord. We are ready for your inspection and you can inspect our unit at any convenient time" replied Sharma looking at the IG's wife. The Chief's wife immediately intervened and told the IG very firmly since it is *Sharavan* Saturday, they should visit the temple first thing in the morning on an empty stomach.

The next morning, I escorted the couple to the temple. At the main entrance Sharmaji, wearing spotlessly white pyjama and kurta with a red *tilak* on his forehead, was standing alongwith the chief priest, and a welcome party comprising of a baby elephant, *Shehnai* and *dholak* players and a bevy of women carrying traditional water pots. As the couple got down from the car, the temple elephant garlanded them, the women performed *'arathi'* and the music party led them into the temple. Sharmaji walked behind the IG's wife with two constables carrying baskets containing fruits, flowers and other *puja* offerings.

The Chief priest performed an elaborate puja for the Lord. We were then taken to the Padmavati temple where special *puja* for the Lord's consort was performed. Here, Sharmaji took out a sari, gave it to the priest saying that it was being gifted to the Goddess by the IG's wife. Madam gave an appreciative look to Sharma.

After the *pujas*, we were led to the office of the temple officer. As we sat down, the priests placed large plantain leaves in front of us and served us steaming hot sweet and *Khara pongal* dripping with pure ghee and curd rice. After partaking the prasadam, the IG started chatting with the chief priest and others and asked them about our unit.

The chief priest said, "Sir, by the grace of the Lord, everything is fine with your unit. Your new commandant is reported to be strict and clean. And you know Sharmaji; he is a great devotee of this temple, and he takes good interest not only in his work, but also in temple affairs."

The IG looked at Sharmaji appreciatively. I uttered a quiet thanks to the Lord, took leave of the IG to be present at the inspection telling Sharma to bring the IG to the unit after he gets back to the Guest House.

The IG arrived with Sharma an hour before lunch, went round the unit, saw some of our records and completed the inspection within an hour expressing his deep satisfaction with our work. While leaving, he patted me at the back. I looked at Sharma. He looked at the photo of Balaji hanging on the wall and folded his hands.

7

Over a (Hot) Cup of Tea

A few decades ago, I was working as the Staff Officer to the Chief in a para-military establishment in New Delhi. The Raising Day of our force was fast approaching and our Chief, the Director General, decided that we should celebrate the day in a befitting manner and asked me to convene a meeting of all concerned. In the meeting the DG said that since after a long time the Raising Day was being held at Delhi, he would invite the Union Minister to inspect the parade, who would give new colours to the force and also give away medals to those who had earned them. The Chief stated that he would seek more facilities to the force from the minister and hence it was necessary for us to impress him.

After the meeting, we all went to the "parade ground" situated in one of our units in Delhi. On seeing the ground, our Chief was disappointed and said that the ground is unimpressive and not suited for such an important occasion. Some of our officers said that since it is centrally located, it would be convenient to have the parade there itself. The DG pondered for a minute and said that if the ground gets a top layer of yellow coloured *Multhani mitti*, it would look better, besides looking nice on TV. He then ordered to procure fifty truckloads of this mud from Punjab, the only nearby place where it was available, and prepare the ground.

By the next week, the ground was really looking nice with the yellow *"Multani Mitti"* surface. The parade rehearsals had begun and the chief was satisfied with the drill. He said that since the drill part of the ceremony had been well taken care of, we should concentrate on the reception and hospitality aspect now. Our young colleague Sharmaji butted in and said. "Sir, please allow me to be in charge of hospitality. I'm experienced in this field as my *mamaji* owns a three star hotel in Shimla." The chief gave an amused look and nodded his agreement.

In the next meeting to review the preparations for the parade, Sharmaji had brought *samosas* from Green Park, *Jalebis* from Bengali Market, and pastries from Hotel Ashok. He asked our boss to taste these samples and give his approval for including them in the menu for the tea being hosted after the parade. When it was time for tea, Sharma produced six different cups of tea stating that two were from Assam, two from Darjeeling, one from Nilgiris and the last a famous blend. Our DG tasted each cup of tea like a veteran tea taster and selected the tea from Assam. He didn't forget to praise Sharma for his meticulous planning.

The Raising Day Parade went off very well and the minister was visibly pleased. Though it was a chilly

November Day in Delhi, the platoons marched very smartly which impressed the minister. When the minister complimented our boss in his speech, the boss could not hide his joy.

After the parade, the chief guest was escorted to the special *shamiana* for tea. Sharmaji welcomed the minister and personally served him refreshments. When it was time to have tea, a bearer in suitable livery, served the Assam tea. The VIP mixed milk and sugar, took one sip and grimaced. He placed the cup on the table and got up saying that the tea is cold. Our DG called for a fresh cup of tea but the minister declined the offer and went away in a huff. The DG's face was red with anger but he didn't utter a word.

The next day, the boss called me to his chamber and said "issue orders transferring Sharma to Duliajan." Being new to the organization, I asked my DG as to where Duliajan is situated. The DG gave a curt look and said, "It is in Assam, the state famous for tea. Sharma will get a lesson or two about serving tea to VIPs if he stays there for a few years". Without uttering a word, I got up saying that I would comply with his orders.

8

Car Without a Steering Wheel

Alarmed by the spurt in road accident cases so soon after I assumed charge as the Police Commissioner of a city, I held an emergency meeting of my subordinates. There was a near unanimous opinion that drunken driving was the main cause. "But how do we detect drunken driver? We don't have breathalysers issued to our unit and if we want to buy them we don't have adequate funds," I said. One officer suggested that for the time being we could use our olfactory nerves for good use. Though it was very unhygienic I agreed very reluctantly.

We started our 'Operation Somras' on a Friday evening. Our officers were told to unobtrusively place themselves at vantage points near clubs and bars, stop all vehicles coming their way and ask the drivers to exhale deeply. If the officer felt that the driver smelt of booze, he would book a case.

A few days later, I had a review meeting. One officer said that on seeing the police party, a drunk made a sudden 'U' turn and fell down from his scooter and hurt himself. Another said that a sozzled car driver vomited when the officer went near him forcing the officer to let him go. A probationary SubInspector said that a well-dressed society lady actually spat on his shirt while exhaling. He didn't know whether it was deliberate or un-intentional. Despite these irritants, it was revealed that the rate of death on roads had actually come down and we decided to continue our good work.

What we thought was our good work was considered unprofessional by our citizens. A few doctors vehemently urged that we should forthwith stop such unhealthy methods of alcohol detection. Some complained that the inspecting cops themselves smelled of booze and they didn't want such close encounters of unhygienic kind. Editorials were written criticizing our ways. One paper wrote, "Bad means for a good end".

I was in a dilemma. I didn't want to stop the operation. At the same time, we did not have funds to buy breathalysers. The Bar Association came to my rescue by gifting a couple of breathalysers. This was a great relief.

The firm which supplied breathalysers, arranged a demo on its use in my office the next day. The demonstrator wanted a volunteer to blow in to the instrument. Inspector Kulkarni, a teetotaler, came forward and blew hard into the mouthpiece. Nothing happened. The assembled officers urged Inspector Patil to test. He vehemently declined. Since Patil was known to have a peg or two before his dinner, everyone wanted him to try.

He reluctantly blew into the machine and it made a beeping sound. Patil was alarmed, and said, "Sir, I had only one peg last night. How can I test positive, this machine is unreliable". The engineers convinced him that he must have had at least six large ones. Patil sheepishly admitted to having a peg too many. We agreed to put the machines to use from that night itself.

Out of curiosity I went on night rounds to see how our officers were using the new machines. While most drivers who had a peg or two admitted their guilt and paid their fines, lots of others picked up quarrels with the officers, but eventually paid their fines. A few drunken drivers abandoned their vehicles on the street and ran away.

At about midnight I received a message over wireless to go near the Club Circle. When I reached there, I saw Asst Sub Inspector (ASI) Timmanna arguing with a person sitting in a car. On seeing this I stopped my vehicle and went there. The moment he saw me, Timmanna gave a smart salute and said. "Look at this gentleman Sir, he has tested positive and is refusing to pay the fine". I looked at the culprit driver quizzically. He said, "Sure Sir, I have had many drinks but why should I pay the fine. I am not driving this car". On hearing this, Timmanna was wild and shouted "Mister, don't tell a lie before my superior officer".

He went towards the gentleman and peeped inside the car and blurted out, "Sir, this car has no steering wheel at all!". The gentleman told the ASI, "Did I not tell you that I am not driving this car?" Timmanna was confused. I asked the car to go. "What Sir, you let off that chap. He admitted having taken drinks and also was driving a car without a steering wheel endangering so many human lives," protested Timmanna.

I smiled and said."Timmanna, in your enthusiasm to catch drunken drivers, you did not observe that the car is a left hand drive vehicle and the driver was sitting next to the drunken owner."

9

Small Savings in England

A few decades ago, when I was selected for a three month long training programme in England, my family members were over-joyed. "Dad, I want a Barbie doll", said my daughter. "Bring me a remote control car", demanded my son. My wife wanted a micro-wave oven for home. "Where do I have so much money for all these? I cannot take more than 500 dollars with me as per our Government regulations," I replied in protest.

"Don't fool us. Your colleague's wife told me that all trainees get four pounds as daily allowance. That makes 360 pounds. Your board and lodge are free. You can easily use the daily allowance to buy the gifts", retorted my wife. To avoid further discussion, I agreed.

Soon I was in the training institution in the UK as part of a batch of twelve officers. The single point agenda of most of us was how to save the maximum amount from our DA so that we could purchase the goods demanded by our family and friends. Bose had determined that he would stop buying booze. Srivastava vowed not to smoke for three months. Kashyap decided not to visit any Indian restaurant but eat the bland food available in our training institution. I decided not to go on sightseeing tours which cost money.

After two weeks, we made a review of whether our resolve had made any difference. Most of us had not spent our DA for unnecessary expenditure. While we were in the midst of our discussions, Muttoo breezed in to say that he went for a haircut and was charged ten pounds. We unanimously decided not to have a haircut while in England to save on our DA.

Next morning during breakfast Sharma looked at Nambi and observed that his hair had grown too long. Nambi said, "Sharmaji I agree I need a haircut, but in UK it is too expensive." Sharma said "who said so? I will cut your hair and you pay me only 4 pounds". Nambi was reluctant. Somehow Sharma persuaded Nambi to get a haircut from him and took Nambi to the terrace of our hostel and gave him a neat scissors cut. Seeing his "Professional" approach, three of our other colleagues also made Sharma cut their hair. Sharma had made a cool pile in the bargain.

Sharma's entrepreneurship gave others similar ideas. Inderjit approached our Course Director the next day and expressed the group's unhappiness on being fed bland English food every day and demanded Indian meals. After a lot of discussion, it was decided that Indu would cook Indian meals for all of us and in return the college would pay him twenty pounds a week. Naturally Sharma, whose motto was to make as many pounds as possible during his stay in England, was envious. He soon demonstrated that no one can beat him in the matter of earning money.

The next Sunday, a local Indian invited us all for *Satyanarayana Pooja* in his house. We all attended, not so much for the *pooja* but for eating authentic Indian food. When the *pooja* was about to begin, the host brought a music player. Sharmaji asked him as to why it was brought.

The host said that as there are not priests nearby, he would play a *pooja* recording he has brought from India and with the help of the recording he would perform *pooja*. Sharmaji gave a deep disappointing look and said, "Brother, why is Sharmaji here for? I am born a *Pandit*, well versed in Vedas, *shastras* and other hindu rituals. Let me be the priest for today's *pooja*". Even before the bewildered host could reply, Sharmaji started off the *mantras* in his deep baritone voice.

When the *pooja* was over, Sharma performed *aarathi* and took *aarathi* plate in front of the gathering. After everyone took the *Aarathi,* he collected all the coins and notes put in the *aarathi* plate by the assembled devotees, and coolly pocketed it. For the service rendered, the host also gave fifty pounds to Sharma. Back in the hostel, Sharma revealed to the bemused batch mates that he had made Ninety pounds within two hours.

Needless to say that till we remained in the UK, Sharma officiated as a priest in local Indian homes every weekend. Did he give up giving haircuts? After the first round, none of us felt like spending four pounds on our haircuts and grew long hair like Beatles.

10

Cattle Station

Soon after I became the police chief of a big city, I received a number of representations about the stray cattle menace. I had also seen cattle sleeping on the middle of the roads hindering the smooth flow of traffic. Deciding to invoke the provision of the Police Act, I directed my subordinates to mercilessly impound stray cattle and clear the streets. A week later, I made a surprise visit to the Town Police Station, to see how my orders were being implemented.

The first thing I noticed after entering the station compound was the "absence" of the station guard. "What a security breach, there is no sentry in this police station," I muttered. As if in answer, I heard a big grunt. A huge black bull was majestically standing on the verandah surveying the road in front. "Sir, when Shiva's *Vahana* is guarding our station, why should there be a sentry?" muttered someone. I turned at the direction of the voice. A police constable was seen amidst half a dozen cows patiently collecting the dung into a basket. He had covered his mouth and nose with a mask normally worn by traffic cops. On seeing me he took off the mask, and saluted me seeking to be forgiven for his remark.

"What are you doing Kempanna?" I asked. "Sir, we have rounded up more than two dozen stray cattle and their owners are not at all keen to pay a fine and take them back. So, we are forced to tie them in the Police station. Since I am the only constable in this Station who can handle cattle, PSI Saab asked me to take care of these guests," said Kempanna.

"Why didn't you send them to the cattle pound?" I asked. "Sir, our Municipal Cattle Pound, not large enough to accommodate all the cows, has refused to accept fresh arrivals," replied the Sub-Inspector who came from inside the PS to receive me.

Before I could think of a solution, I heard a loud shriek. From the back of the police station, a Head Constable in full uniform came running out. His pants were torn and he was bleeding. He came to me and pleaded to be sent to the hospital.

I agreed and asked him the cause of his injury. He replied, "Sir, I have put in twenty years in this department and have learnt to turn many a situations to my pecuniary advantage. When you ordered rounding up of cattle in the city, I saw a great opportunity. I thought my family will have thick milk to feed our kids and also make some extra money by selling the surplus to the canteen nearby."

"Last night, when my colleagues bought two nice Sindhi cows to the police station, I looked at their udders and thought that I could get at least 15 litres of milk a day. Sometime ago, I went to milk one of the cows. The moment

I placed a bucket below the udders and squatted to milk her, the cow kicked me." Interjecting at this juncture, the PSI said, "Sir, unlike this HC, PC Kempanna is not greedy. He was content collecting only the dung and sell it as "*Berrani*" (dried dung cake used as fuel). Our HC paid a price for his greed. It is a good lesson to him."

I withdrew my orders of impounding stray cattle forthwith.

11

The King's Gift

The very first time, I received an official gift from a foreigner was when I performed security duties with an Emir from the Gulf. For three days, I lived in the same hotel as the King lived and went wherever he went. However, since he did not know English our communication was through his Police Chief.

On the last day of his visit, the Emir called me and gave me an envelope stating that it is his gift for me. When I found that the envelope contained 1000 crisp US dollar notes, I promptly went to the Emir's room and returned the envelope. The Emir was puzzled. I told his Police Chief it is not only improper but also demeaning to accept cash gifts. The Police Chief said, "Sir, by returning the gift you have insulted our King." I said that I would be very happy to get an autographed photo of the Emir as my gift. The Police Chief communicated my desire to the Emir, who promptly gave me an autographed photo of himself.

After fifteen minutes, the Police Chief called me again and said, "Sir, my boss is feeling bad that you did not accept his gift. You must accept something from him." So saying, he took me to the Emir's room. This time the Emir gave me a small packet. I could not ask him what it contained since it was time for the Emir's departure and I saw him off.

I came back to my room and on opening the packet found a gleaming Swiss watch. When I returned home, I kept the watch in my safe. I did not wear the watch but kept on opening its box once a year to re-live the memories of the Gulf king who by then had been dethroned in his country. Two decades passed this way.

One day, my daughter forced me to wear the watch. It did not work. My wife persuaded me to get it repaired and wear it. We found a reputed watch dealer who agreed to repair it.

After two days, I went to collect the watch. The repairer demanded Rs.2000 as his charge. My heart shrunk. I said "Look Sir, this watch does not even cost Rs.200 and you are asking Rs.2000 for its repair. You might as well keep it yourself".

He asked me from where I procured this watch. I told him that it was a King's gift, a quarter of a century ago. The repairer said, "Sir! Will any King gift useless junk? This is a precious piece which will fetch you a fortune if you sell it. Keep it as a heirloom. My repair charge is nothing when compared to the value of this watch."

I paid Rs.2000 without fuss and started wearing the King's gift from the same day. Even now, I do not know its price. But I know what I wear on my wrist is priceless.

12

Gratitude is Still Alive

Serving in the police department for more than three decades and seeing crime at close quarters, I have realized that gratitude is a rare commodity in today's world. Since it is rare, I have always made it a point to remember the help rendered to me by others, tending to forget instances of help given by me. A recent incident has made me change my view.

One day, a middle aged person wearing shorts and T-shirt entered my office chamber, along with his young son. I thought him to be an NRI and did not hesitate to show my displeasure for barging into my office without announcement that too in casual attire. He popped up his visiting card which proclaimed that he is working as a doctor in USA. I asked him to make the visit short as I was busy at that moment. He said, he has come to India on a holiday to see his mother in his hometown of Hyderabad and came to Bangalore only to meet me and to thank me. I was flummoxed and raised by eyebrows. I told him that I don't remember ever meeting him. He said, "Sir! you are very right. We have not at all met before and are strangers to each other. But only because of you, I am able to pursue my career in the US peacefully."

Becoming curious, I asked him to explain. He asked me whether I know a senior IPS officer from Andhra Pradesh. When I replied in the affirmative, he said that he had approached me through that officer two years ago seeking my help and I had obliged. When I said I was not able to recall what help I had rendered, he said that his family had property dispute with a person living in Bangalore. His widowed mother, who was living alone in Bangalore and terribly worried, had approached the Police Officer in Hyderabad. After my intervention in the matter, the dispute had been resolved, he said. I did not remember the incident in question, but I pretended to remember the incident and asked him how come he is meeting me after two years of the incident.

He said that though he wanted to call and thank me, he wanted to actually see the stranger who had helped his family in flesh and blood. Being a busy doctor practicing in America, he could not find time to come to India. When told that he could have simply sent me a Thank You Card, he said meeting his benefactor in person, means a lot to him.

I was really touched by his gesture. He got up and asked me whether he could give a hug to me. He was hesistant since I was in my uniform. I got up, went near him and said "go ahead" After giving me a tight hug, he made his son shake my hands and give me a big box of candies. When I thanked the doctor, he said that his police friend in Andhra had informed him that I am a freelance writer. I smiled. He then opened his bag and gave me a beautiful pen as a gift saying, "Sir! your help meant a lot to me and my family. Since you meet so many people you have forgotten about this help. At least, this pen will make you remember me forever".

I use the pen every day and remember that 'gratitude' is still alive.

13

Occupational Hazard

Inspector Ram was leisurely reading the day's newspaper since no processions or protests were slated for the day. On hearing a click of heels, he looked up and saw constable Lakshman. Giving a smart salute, Lakshman said, "Sir, my daughter's marriage is fixed next week and I need to go on leave". Ram got angry and asked, "Are you telling the truth, or planning your leave as a part of police protest?" Lakshman immediately took out a marriage invitation from a bunch and handed over one to his boss.

"I know one can get invitations printed for a mere Rs.100. Your leave is rejected" said Ram. Lakshman touched his boss' feet saying, "Sir, why should I lie? Send anyone to my native place and ascertain the truth". Ram did not budge and said, "You may talk to Dy Commissioner of Police (DCP) and get his permission"

The next day, the jurisdictional DCP summoned Ram to his office, and shouted, "Are you not capable of handling your subordinates? Do you think your DCP has no other work but grant leave to your constables?" "Sir, it is not like that, I was directed not to grant leave to any one during the proposed police strike. When I refused leave, Lakshman has approached you". The DCP was placated. On his return to the Station, Ram gave a mouthful to Lakshman and forgot this episode.

The next morning, a surprise was awaiting Inspector Ram. Except two Head Constables, everyone had reported sick. Ram called the HC and sought the reason. "As a protest against your inhuman attitude towards Lakshman, all our colleagues have absented", said the HC. Ram asked the HC to alert the higher ups.

Within an hour, Ram was summoned by the Joint Police Commissioner and served the order of his suspension for not handling his subordinates tactfully. A dejected Ram went home and explained the situation to his wife who was furious.

The next day, when the Police Commissioner was in his office attending to his work, a woman was ushered before him. Without much ado, the lady asked the reason why her husband Ram was unjustly suspended. The Commissioner lost his temper and told her that she cannot interfere in Departmental matters. Hearing these words, the woman said, "I can't tolerate such injustice to my husband. I shall commit suicide and declare that you are responsible for it". In a matter of seconds, she took out a bottle, emptied its contents into her mouth and fell down. The Commissioner was aghast. He got the lady shifted to a nearby hospital and within minutes, he revoked the suspension of Inspector Ram.

A beaming Ram came back to his police station the next day. As he started his day's work, Lakshman approached him again and sought leave. The Inspector was furious, shouted at him and asked him to get out. Hearing this, Lakshman took out a bottle and saying that he is disgusted with his life poured kerosene on himself and before he could be stopped, lit a match stick. Very soon Lakshman was rushed to the hospital.

Inspector Ram was suspended again.

Note: In 2016, a spate of suicides by police officers rattled Karnataka, and some unscrupulous cops would threaten their senior officers with suicide to get their demands met. The above article is against that background

14

Bitten by Publicity

The Superintendent of Police was very happy. At last, his force had been sanctioned a 'dog squad' like others. He could now proudly announce to the community, he was serving that - with the help of trained police dogs many serious crimes in the district would be detected. He called his subordinates for a meeting to discuss how to make this a big media event.

The Inspector in charge of the dog squad informed that the police headquarters has allotted three dogs, Kamla, Vimla and Sindhu, all German Shepherds, and that the dogs have already arrived, and that their kennels have also been constructed in the police lines. He added that while Kamla and Vimla were procured as pups and trained, Sindhu, which is three year old, came on transfer from another district. The Deputy SP suggested that since the Minister in-charge of the district was visiting the town next week, it would be appropriate if the Minister dedicates the services of the dog squad to the public. This suggestion was unanimously welcomed and the meeting discussed how to make the function impressive and get appreciation from the minister. Every detail was minutely chalked out.

Invitations for the function were sent to all the prominent citizens. The State Police Chief had agreed to visit the district and preside over the function. On the D-Day, the minister arrived at the parade ground on time. He was received by the DGP and taken to the saluting base. A big police contingent marched past and the dogs in their colourful new uniforms were the cynosure of all eyes. After the march past, the dog handlers brought the dogs to the Centre of the ground and made them perform various tasks like sitting, kneeling, saluting, marching, barking, etc.,

Later the dogs displayed how they would detect criminals by the very scent of the item left at the scene of offence. The Inspector made a policeman to keep his handkerchief on the ground, and a dog after sniffing the handkerchief came smelling the ground and finally caught the arm of the constable. The entire audience loudly clapped and appreciated. After this, the dogs showed how they guard prisoners and how they obey the commands of only their handlers and none else.

The Minister was thoroughly impressed by this display and after the parade was over, he expressed his desire to go near the dogs and pat them to show his appreciation. The SP signalled to the dog squad inspector. The three dogs were made to stand in line. The minister walked towards them. The first two dogs 'shook hands' with the minister. When he went near the third dog, it suddenly jumped on the minister and held his right arm firmly. Everyone was aghast. With great difficulty, the dog handler got the minister released from dog's clutches. The SP and the DGP rushed the bleeding minister to the Hospital. After administering first aid and the mandatory injections the Minister left the district in a huff to the State headquarters.

The SP was very much worried. He summoned the Inspector of the dog squad and sought an explanation. The Inspector said "Sir, Sindhu comes from the district which is home to the honourable minister. How should I know that she would recognize the Minister even after all the theft cases against him were acquitted in the courts?"

The SP was speechless.

15

Vanishing Trick

I was just promoted as Deputy Inspector General Police of a Police range consisting of four districts. Since I had not served in any of those districts earlier, it was a new experience for me. On assuming charge, I met all the senior officers and exhorted them to be people friendly. "One of the ways to attract people to visit police stations without fear is to change the police station environment. If we keep the surroundings of our police stations clean and inviting, people will not hesitate to visit us." I said, adding that having a nice garden outside the police station building would definitely attract the public.

Since my love for horticulture was by then well known, it did not take long for my new colleagues to quickly learn how to please me. Within the next three months, most of my subordinates had raised small gardens in their office premises. However, since one of the districts under me was perennially drought hit, the horticultural efforts of those officers had been in vain.

I had to inspect a police station in the drought hit district. As my car reached the police station gate, I was led to the guard of honour line up. The Police Sub Inspector (PSI) and his men were well turned out and presented a good drill. I was happy. After taking the salute, I was surprised to see an excellent rose garden in front of the building. A beautiful green lawn had been laid and there were colourful roses all round. I was extremely pleased that even in such a drought hit area a lovely garden had been nurtured.

When I asked the officer in charge the secret of growing roses in such an area he replied that he had got a bore well dug which yielded good quantities of water and replaced the top soil. Since the exterior of the Police Station had made me happy, I did not bother to check in to the finer points of the police station work and gave a clean chit to the officer.

A month later, a double murder took place in the same area. Since I had to visit the scene of the crime, I took along with me an IPS probationer as part of his practical training. After the visit, I told the probationer about the excellent rose garden raised in the nearby Police Station. The probationer who was an MSc in Horticulture said that growing roses in the soil found in that area was almost impossible. He was keen to know the technique adopted and asked me to take him there.

After about a half-an-hours' drive we both were in front of the police station. Except for a head constable and a sentry there was no one else in the PS. As I got down from the car I noticed that something was amiss. The probationer asked me, "Sir, where are the roses?" There were neither rose plants nor the lush green lawn in front of the Police

Station. I was taken aback. The probationer said that I must have brought him to some other Police Station by mistake. I vehemently asserted that I could not be wrong and asked the Head Constable where the roses had gone. While he was mumbling for a reply, the Station House Officer arrived. On seeing me, he started shivering and sweating. When I asked him about the roses, he prostrated and holding my feet firmly said, "Sir, please excuse me. Knowing your fondness for horticulture, I knew you would rate me well if I grew a good garden. My brother who is a horticulture officer embedded rose pots in the soil just before your visit. After you left, the plants were returned."

As we were leaving the premises, I told the probationer, "This is the greatest vanishing trick I have ever seen in my life."

16

Minister's Footwear

Having been promoted as an SP, I was placed in charge of a small but communally sensitive district. Soon after assuming charge I visited all the police stations and most places of interest in the district. In a corner of the district was a temple of Goddess Durga situated inside a cave. This temple was attracting a large number of devotees from far and wide.

Though buses would ply up to the temple town, facilities for pilgrims were meager. There was a *dharmshala* where free board and lodging were available to the pilgrims. On new moon days lots of pilgrims would visit the temple and we had to post policemen there. Makeshift shops selling flowers, *pooja* materials and the like would spring up outside the temple every new moon day and vanish soon after.

Within three months of my assuming charge, general elections were announced and a new party came to power. An MLA from my district was made a minister and was given an important portfolio. Since I had developed very good relations with the new minister, I was elated. At once I phoned him and congratulated him. He was beaming with happiness and said that he would visit the district very soon. A few days later he called to say that he would be visiting the district the next day and would visit the cave temple. "You see, I am a staunch devotee of the Devi and as I also am the MLA of that area, I must visit the temple and pay my obeisance", he said. When I reminded him that the next day was not the new moon day, he replied, "For thanksgiving days don't matter."

I met the minister at the district border along with the Collector and we drove straight to the temple. Hundreds of his followers received him on his arrival at the temple town shouting slogans and bursting crackers. The minister made an impromptu speech and went into the temple with his supporters.

We waited outside. After about 15 minutes the local Sub-Inspector came to me with a grim face, and said: "Sorry to inform this sir, but someone has stolen the minister's chappals, which had been left outside the temple." I asked him to go to the nearest footwear shop and buy a new pair and keep them outside. The officer said, "Sir, the closest footwear shop is 30 km away and by the time I return, the Hon'ble *Mantriji* would have left the district.

The Collector interjected! "Don't worry SP *Saab*, hundreds of pairs of footwear have been deposited outside the temple. Let your constables search for footwear identical to the ones used by the minister and keep them where the minister had kept them." I nodded in agreement at this fool-proof solution. My officer said, "Sir, it is not possible. You see Sir, our minister *saab* wears size 12 chappals and there are no chappals of that size here to replace his."

At the juncture my Deputy Superintendent of Police said, "The best thing is to get a new pair from outside. I have already sent a wireless message. A new pair should be on its way sir." I gave him an appreciative glance.

Meanwhile the Inspector said, "Sir, what if the new pair does not reach in time? The minister will shout that if the police cannot even take care of his slippers how they can protect the lives and properties of citizens. Sir, I am sure to be suspended and you will be transferred!"

Meanwhile, the Police Control room informed us that nowhere in the district could they find a size 12 pair of footwear. I got panicky. Soon, the minister came out of the temple. I was sweating profusely. Since I wanted to own the responsibility for the mishap, I went to him, smartly saluted and said: "Sir a serious problem is at hand."

He asked, "What is the problem? Is there a police firing in the district or do we have a communal clash?"

I explained what had happened.

He started guffawing and said, "SP *Saab*, losing footwear in this temple is considered a very good omen by us, locals. I am definitely going to last five years as minister". And he shook my hands.

I looked at the Collector. He winked.

17

Royal Repast Festivity

On the first day of my practical training as in-charge Circle Inspector, the local Deputy Superintendent of Police invited me for breakfast. I requested for Idli-Vada. As I finished eating, the DSP said, "Sir! we are in Hyderabad-Karnataka and the traditional breakfast here is Kichadi with *Keema.* It is good for health and you should try it." I reluctantly agreed.

And a large portion of kichadi, a boiled egg and a bowl of *Keema* was served. Meanwhile the DSP had ordered *"jolada rotis"* (Chapatis made with jowar) with omlette for himself, and asked me to share the same.

I felt full and refused more food. But, the DSP went ahead with *Chow Chow Bath* and fruits.

"Sir! in Police work one should eat breakfast like a King, as you never know where you would be able to get your lunch and when you get your lunch you should eat it like a Prince. If you don't get your lunch, you will not have regrets since you would have had a good breakfast. And your dinner should be like a pauper. Let this be your first lesson," the DSP suggested.

As we sipped our coffee, there was a message from the Police Control Room that a group clash had taken place in a village 30 kms away and two had died. On our way to the scene of offence, the DSP said "Sir! the second lesson is that you should not only have a royal breakfast, but should also carry some eatables with you whenever you leave your residence." He had kept some *"khadak Jolada rotis* (hard jowar rotis akin to *khakras*)", biscuits, Chutney powders and water in his jeep.

We reached the crime spot after an hour of bumpy ride and learnt the details of the incident from the police *patel.* By the time we got the case registered and completed other formalities and admitted the injured to the hospital, it was past 2 pm. I was hungry.

The DSP asked his driver to open the lunch box and take out the crispy *rotis.* We consumed the *rotis* along with onion and chilies provided by the police *patel.* The district Superintendent of Police came to the village around 5 pm and directed me to camp there till we arrested a few accused.

I wasn't prepared for the night-halt in the village but the DSP remained silent.

By 8 pm, I was both hungry and sleepy. The DSP asked the police *patel* to get the village school opened. We joined a few benches to make them our cot. Since we had exhausted the crispy *rotis* for lunch, and biscuits during the evening there was nothing left to eat. Seeing the police all the villagers had deserted the village and there was nothing available in the village.

When the DSP offered to send his jeep to the neighbouring town to get us some food, I reminded him that, "One should dine like a pauper, DSP Saab".

18

Prestige Regained

It was my first posting as Asst. Superintendent of Police of a Sub-Division. I received a message that the range DIG was intending to inspect a police station under my jurisdiction. The DIG was known to be a no-nonsense officer and was prone to keep under suspension officers who didn't perform well.

Inspection camps those days would last for three days and officers would camp for at least two nights in the place of inspection. We were happy to learn that my DIG was coming with his wife, which meant that the inspection will not drag on till late night.

Finishing his work at 5 pm on the first day, the DIG told me that his wife wanted to go for a movie and gave me money to book the tickets. Keen that no policeman should accompany them, he asked me for pick them up from the Guest House and drop them back after the movie. When I went to the movie hall to pick them back, he was dull and later his wife told me that someone had picked his purse which contained about Rs.900.

I called an emergency meeting of the Inspectors and subordinate staff in my office and disclosed the bad news. The Sub-Inspector of the police station under inspection thought that the DIG would suspend him for not keeping the criminals under check and his chances of promotion were bleak. While everyone agreed with him, a Circle Inspector offered to solve the case.

After breakfast the next morning, the Inspector greeted the DIG with a grand salute and told him the man who picked his pocket the previous evening was caught. The" culprit " was then ceremonially produced before the DIG. The lanky teenager admitted his crime and said that he threw away the purse, spent Rs.100 on food and drinks and handed over rest of money back to the Inspector.

The DIG praised the Inspector for his "excellent and super-fast detection" and said that he would reward the Inspector suitably. The Inspector told the DIG that since no complaint has been lodged, he would book a "petty case" against the pickpocket and release him.

After the DIG left, I called the Inspector aside and asked him how he could solve the case so fast. "Sir! the thief you saw is a known pickpocket of our town, but he did not pick the DIG's pocket. All of us officers pooled in some cash, gave it to the thief and asked him to confess to the crime. If we had returned the entire amount lost, the recovery would have looked unnatural", the Inspector said. He not only saved our prestige, but also of the DIG's.

19

Recovery Police Style

I was then working in Delhi in a Central Police Force, on deputation. While on a holiday in my home-town, a classmate of mine invited me over to his place for tea. A Deputy Commissioner of Police (DCP), a common friend, was the other invitee. Since it was raining, we had an extended tea session. When the rain stopped, we both took leave of the host to return home.

The DCP requested me to drop him home as he had sent his official vehicle away. I had parked my old Premier Padmini car on the road. As I opened the door, I noticed that a burglar had broken into the car and had stolen the tape-recorder fitted in it. The rains had given the thief a good cover. I was aghast. Addressing the DCP, I said, "Look both of us are senior police officers. Is it not ironical that I should be a victim of a theft, and that too in your jurisdiction, when both of us were socializing?"

The DCP, who was visibly embarrassed, muttered, "I am sorry about the theft. Please lodge a complaint. We will do our best to recover what was stolen". I said, "My friend, you are as much aware as I am that there is no chance of recovering my car stereo system. Why do you want me to lodge a complaint and add this to the long list of undetected cases in your town? Even if you do succeed, do you think I will come all the way from Delhi to depose in the court, spending more money on my travel than what the lost stereo costs?" I started the car, telling the DCP to forget the incident.

I dropped the DCP off and returned home. An hour later, the phone rang. The Assistant Commissioner of Police (Crime)(ACP) was the caller.

He said, "Sir! I am sorry to learn that your car stereo was stolen. Even though you have decided not to lodge a complaint, we shall leave no stone unturned to retrieve what was stolen". I wished him good luck.

The next morning an Asst. Sub Inspector (ASI) and a Head Constable (HC) from the Crime Branch came home. Giving me a smart salute, the ASI said, "Sir! we caught a notorious burglar an hour ago. He had a number of car stereos with him. Our ACP asked us to show you the stereo systems and to find out if any of them belongs to you". The HC opened a gunny sack and took out three car stereos. I looked at them and said that none of them was mine. With great disappointment, the duo went back.

That evening, the ACP himself came home. He said, "Sir! we have cracked your case. Our team picked up an inter-state criminal when he was disposing of some stolen goods. They found your car stereo in his possession". So saying, the ACP opened his briefcase and placed on my table a lovely Sony car stereo. I looked at him and said, "Friend, I am sorry to disappoint you. My car is an old Premier Padmini and my stereo was made locally. This is a Sony and does not belong to me."

The ACP was startled. Recovering his composure soon, he said, "Sir, I knew that this set did not belong to you. But I am certain that it is a stolen system. The owner of this stereo system has preferred not to lodge a complaint and in this vast city, there is no chance of locating him. We both know that your set was lost. If you do not accept this piece as yours, it will get consigned to the Lost Property Room and become junk in six months. No one will be happy if that happens."

So saying, he got his driver to fit the "Sony" stereo system in my car. I was a mute spectator.

Did the ACP's logic prevail over my conscience? I stil' have no answer.

20

Swalpa Adjust Maadi

It was a very hot day in Delhi. I was to report for duty on deputation as a Staff Officer in Central Para Military Force. I was full of trepidation. Here I was in the national capital, along with wife and two kids, a young SP uprooted from his home State, not knowing how offices in the Central Government work, worried about finding a home and admitting children in new schools.

Since I did not know anyone in my 'new' office, I phoned the officer in charge of the Force control room and sought directions to reach my office. He promised to send a vehicle. Meanwhile, I wore my ceremonial wollen uniform. Soon a police constable appeared in my room, and said "*Gaadi tayar hai saab*"!

The constable brought a shining black motorcycle to the portico and asked me to ride pillion. I was aghast. My wife wondered as to how I could travel on a motorcycle wearing my wollen ceremonial uniform. She told the constable that I was having two official cars in my previous posting as District SP. The Constable said, "Madam! in our Force only DIG and above are entitled for four wheelers. All officers of *Saab's* rank in Delhi have to travel in DTC buses, that too standing. *Thoda adjust karna* madam. He will get used to it". I adjusted to riding a two wheeler till I secured an official apartment.

Soon, I was allotted a 'transit flat' in Pragati Vihar housing complex, situated a few yards from my office. I brought my family to have a look at our new abode. As we entered the house, my wife's jaws fell. "This flat has only one small bedroom. What will we do if we have guests? We had such a huge bungalow with five rooms, servants' quarters and a garden with swimming pool to boot. Did you opt for deputation only to make us suffer?", she cried. I consoled her saying, "Look at the advantages we have. This furnished flat is so centrally located that my office, schools and markets are close by. I don't have to ride pillion on a motorcycle anymore. We have twenty four hour water and power. Besides, this is only transit flat, we will soon get a three bedroom flat. Till then *swalpa adjust madona*"(Let us adjust a little). The family reluctantly moved into the new flat the next day.

By the time we moved into the flat, admissions in all prestigious schools in Delhi had closed. Kendriya Vidyalaya was our only hope. That too, only the Kendriya Vidyalaya nearest to my home could admit our children. The nearest school was in the Pragati Vihar campus itself! With children in tow, my wife and I went in search of the school the next day. At one corner of our complex, we saw a row of tents with a huge signage on which was written "K.V.Pragati Vihar". My wife and children were so shocked they were speechless. After some time my wife said, "Look, when you said we cannot admit our children to famous schools in Delhi this year, I consoled myself saying we have a chance next year. When you said we have to settle for Kendriya Vidyalaya, I agreed. How can I agree to admit our kids in this tented school in this hot climate?" I told her, *"Swalpa adjust madikobeku.* After all it is a question of only eight months more. Next year we will admit them in a good school". With great reluctance she agreed.

While we were getting adjusted to our new environs, we started getting regular stream of close relatives opting to stay with us. It was a great strain, but we would tell our guests, *"swalpa adjust madikolli"* and tried to be good hosts. Some of our guests who were close kith and kin were greatly inconvenienced since I had no vehicle. I was therefore forced to buy a car. This meant taking our guests around Delhi which was a big pain. My wife would say *"swalpa adjust maadi"* and I would swallow my anger.

After the "Guest season" was over, I was allotted a house in a prestigious locality in Delhi. It was one step below my entitlement but was having servants quarters and garage, two luxuries every officer in Delhi looks for. We all went to see the house. It was an old house, situated very near a famous public school. Our neighbours were big shots. I was quite happy and asked my wife as to when we could move to our new abode

"In these past few months, we all are having lunch together since your office and children's school are located so near home. Since you almost have an office-cum-residence, I don't feel lonely. Our neighbours are all very friendly and kids have also adjusted to their 'tent school'. If we move to this house we have to spend a lot on transportation. Only during the visits of guests, we are inconvenienced. But all our guests are close relatives or friends. They will adjust. Since we have already adjusted a little, why not adjust some more and stay in Pragati Vihar flat itself?"

I was speechless

Note: *Swalpa Adjust Maadi/Madikolli* in Kannada language mean" Please Adjust a Little". It is a typical Kannada expression, commonly used in all walks of life

21

Like Poles Repel

I have learnt to be suspicious about people by my training as a Police Officer. But I had never felt that I could evoke suspicion, until I started travelling abroad. While trying to walk out of the green channel at Heathrow airport a couple of years ago, a customs official pulled me aside and started questioning. He made me open my suitcase and his eye caught a bottle containing a red powder. Though I explained it as *chutney* powder, which we Indians mix with our food, he opened the container lid and took a deep breath. As expected he was seized by a bout of uncontrolled sneezing which made his colleagues rush to him and subject me to further intense interrogation. Finally, when I was allowed to go, my ego was fully deflated.

I had to pass through the same airport three months later. Thinking that the UK customs had forgotten me, I passed through the green channel along with a friend. I was once again detained, though I was not carrying *chutney* powder this time around. I was questioned for twenty minutes and my bags were thoroughly checked. When I was allowed to go, my friend remarked that there must be something in me that arouses suspicion among the Brits. I agreed and laughed it off.

A few years later, I visited New York with my wife. The moment we crossed immigration, an authoritative looking uniformed woman came to us and asked us to step aside. Since it was our first US visit, we were carrying a number of eatables, including *chutney* powder, for our hosts. When the lady officer confiscated all the food items, tears came rushing to my wife's eyes. It took all my skills to convince the woman that we are not smugglers and we are not carrying any contraband.

On our return journey, we had a break in Paris. When we went to the airport to board our flight, we were stopped at the entrance by two security persons and were questioned for ten minutes. They knew very little English and we knew no French. After they allowed us inside, we were subjected to further checks at least twice. Fed up with this treatment, I revealed that I am a police officer from India. The moment they heard the word, 'police' they segregated me, took me to a separate room and started questioning me further! In the meantime, boarding for the flight had started and my wife was getting tense. At last, I managed to board. My wife was upset. I explained that because of 'racial profiling', such things do happen and not to worry over it.

I took her to Thailand later. On our way home, at Bangkok airport, I was singled out by security and searched for ten minutes! As I joined her, my wife remarked 'Is this also a case of racial profiling?' I said 'No, this is a case of people in the same profession easily spotting their colleagues'. She agreed and said 'like poles always repel'.

22

Sparrows in a Distant Land

When I was a child, a lot of birds especially sparrows would visit our kitchen and search for small food particles. When my grandmother used to clean rice, a number of them would be around her to collect the grains of rice falling on the floor. Slowly as Bangalore became a concrete jungle, they simply vanished, making me fondly remember them off and on.

I visited Disneyland at Hong Kong recently. Midway through I wanted a break. When my wife and children went to see a show, I found a bench beneath a shady tree. I sat there, opened my tiffin, took out a slice of bread smeared with chutney powder and started eating. Soon two sparrows came near me and stood at a distance. Thrilled to see these long lost friends, I passed on a small bread crumb at them. Both fought for the piece, but only one could get it. I felt pity on the second sparrow and passed on another crumb for him. Soon dozens of sparrows landed near me from nowhere. I began throwing crumbs of bread at them. They would dive and catch the piece before it fell on the ground. Keeping the piece in their little beaks, they would take off not allowing the bread crumb to be snatched away by others. Those that didn't get the bread, would longingly look at my hands. The event was exciting and I enjoyed every minute of it.

Meanwhile the sight of me feeding sparrows attracted the attention of many passersby. A woman with a small child in a stroller came near me, handing over a packet of biscuits to feed the sparrows. She entertained her child and took my photos.

Soon the biscuits were gone and more and more sparrows were hovering by. The only food item left was a packet of "Congress" peanuts, I had brought from Bangalore. When one small piece of nut fell on the ground, a sparrow slowly got near it, smelt it, picked it in its small beak and flew away. Soon more sparrows landed. I made small pieces of peanuts and started feeding again.

I did not know how the time passes. Meanwhile, a big crowd had gathered around me. Some were taking pictures. My wife who had come back from the show was worried as to why so many had gathered around me. She elbowed her way to my bench and when she saw what was happening, she muttered: "Now I know why you don't want to see the sights of Disneyland. These sparrows must have migrated from Bangalore. That's why they are enjoying the "*Congress Kadale Kayi*" and you want to be with your long lost friends!"

Kadlekai means peanut in Kannada and Congress peanut is a special masala peanut, typically made in Karnataka

23

Modelling Blues

As I was enjoying my evening walk in a park, I felt a tap on my shoulder. A young fellow, pointing towards his camera asked me, "Sir, can I take your picture?" Being pleasantly surprised I replied, "Look, I don't know who you are. I am past my prime and am least interested in getting my mug shot taken". He said, "Sir I am a professional photographer. We are in search of models of your age for a big advertising campaign. If you agree, I will take you picture now."

As a policeman, I never agree to the request of strangers and told him that I would contact him the next day. Thus, I took his contact details and continued my walk.

After I returned home, I told my wife and children my tryst with the unknown photographer. I told my wife, "You are always criticizing my looks. I have always maintained that I am as handsome as Dev Anand. Merely watching my looks and gait, an unknown photographer has felt that I am a fit enough to be a model. Very soon you will see my pictures in all glossy magazines and newspapers." While my wife continued to be skeptical, both my children were enthusiastic saying that they hoped to see their father on hoardings and television. They forced me to call the photographer immediately and fix up an appointment.

I called the photographer and he asked me to come to Bangalore Palace the next day for a photo shoot. The next morning, I had a clean haircut and shampooed my hair. Wearing my best suit, I dragged my wife to accompany me to the photo shoot.

At the palace, the photographer received us and asked me to go to the changing room. I was made to wear a nice embroidered Kurta with a Bengali type dhoti. I surmised that the advertisers want me to promote Indian dress. A young girl made up my face and commented that I was looking very handsome. I literally blushed. When I arrived at the location, the photographer brought a six year old girl and asked me to lift her high in the air. I protested saying that I agreed for the photo shoot because I thought it was a solo ad and I don't want others in the picture frame.

The photographer turned serious and said, "Sir, we are now shooting for *chyavanprash* ad. You will fit the role of a healthy grandfather in the ad". My wife, who heard this, started laughing aloud. Being very upset at this turn of events, I returned home without taking part in the shoot.

24

Staying Young: A Day Dreaming

I believed in the old adage that a man is as old as he feels and a woman as old as she looks. When strands of grey appeared on my pate, I wasn't overly worried. I maintained that after all getting old is a natural phenomenon and one should not go against the tide.

One evening my son's friend came home for dinner and as we were talking, he asked whether I had retired from service. Since I had almost 10 years to reach the retirement age, I told him so. But I started wondering whether I am looking older than my age. My wife suggested I could get my hair dyed and get a facial done, but I vehemently opposed her suggestion. One of my friends attempted to dye his hair and actually got into his death bed because of some chemical reaction.

A few years later, I went to my school re-union and met many of my class fellows. One of them remarked to others that I am having a distinguished look. I asked him whether he meant that I am looking old. His silence was revealing and once again a thought came to me to make an attempt to look young.

Sometime later, I attended a wedding. When I went to wish the bride, her mother directed the newlyweds to touch my feet asking them to take the blessings of a grandfather. I was visibly embarrassed as both my children were still in college and I had not even thought of their marriage. My wife reasoned that our first child is already 20 years old and had she got married at the legally permissible marriage age, we would have definitely become grandparents. Hearing that explanation, I didn't bother much over the matter.

The other day, I was a chief guest for an important function and the media covered it extensively. One newspaper reported that I am a retired officer. I got annoyed and spoke to the editor whom I had known since childhood. He apologized for the faux paus, but gently reminded me that had the government not increased the retirement age. I would have naturally retired from service by then. I was speechless.

As I sat brooding over the editor's comments, I received an email from a friend which said that life is not measured by the breaths we take but by the moments that take our breaths away. Remembering such moments, I realized that I still have the energy of a middle-aged man and am free from ailments people of my age suffer from. I am still a teenager in my thoughts.

25

Watching a Tragic Play

I went to witness a play which was being staged as part of a drama festival 'Bengaluru Habba' recently. Since the famous actor couple Nazeeruddin and Rathna-Shah was doing the main roles, I had not bothered to know the name of the play; the hall was only half full. I wondered aloud how such famous actors could not pull crowds. My neighbour informed me that the play being staged was 'Antigone'. I thought Bangalore audiences may not be interested in watching tragedies, that too Greek ones. After all Greek and Latin are difficult to comprehend.

Having been a student of literature, and having studied 'Antigone' as part of my syllabus, I was eager to see the play unfold on stage. The announcement that the play was not in its original form but was adapted to suit Indian audience dampened me a bit. When the curtains opened an actor playing a palace guard came on stage, chased a person in the audience for speaking on the cellphone, took him on stage and 'executed him'. There was a big guffaw at this not so subtle message not to use cellphones. This scene did not help set the mood for a tragic play.

My thoughts went back to the day Prof. Menezes taught us Greek tragedy. He quoted Aristotle stating that tragedy is an imitation of action that is serious, complete and of a certain magnitude. What the guard did on the stage was frivolous and was not supposed to be the introduction of a tragic play. Prof. Menezes had also taught us that tragedies should have 'comic interludes' to help lighten the somber mood. But can the interlude be the beginning of the play, I wondered. I was taught that pity and fear are the main ingredients of a Greek tragedy.

In the scenes that unfolded, I did not feel pity or fear for any of the characters who were on stage. I had learnt that one of the ingredients of Greek tragedy is spectacle. The Spartan stage décor was least spectacular. Probably the Mumbai team could not afford to mount costly 'sets' in Bangalore.

Aristotle had said that if a person witnesses a tragedy, he should have a purgatory experience; he should identify himself with the central character, mentally undergo the same agony and thereby feel lighter after watching the play. I never felt either elevated or purgated after seeing the play at Bangalore. However, I was amazed that I could recite verbatim what Prof. Menezes had taught me about Greek tragedy 39 years ago. I came back from the hall feeling happy and not tragic!

26

Dogged Perseverance: A Positive Conversion of Arrogance

Since childhood, I had a morbid fear of dogs. When I was a student I have been chased by these four legged creatures any number of times. Maybe they always thought that I had nice calves to chew on. Thankfully, no dog managed to bite me. Probably because whenever I would see a dog, I would make a very quick U-turn and be as far away as possible from him.

When I was engaged to be married, I learnt that my fiancée was very fond of dogs. All her life she had lived with dogs and days before our engagement, her fourth dog died. Only her imminent marriage had made her come out of her mourning. But she couldn't help thinking about her pet most of the time. Soon after our honeymoon, we set up family in a remote rural area. We had a big bungalow with a number of people around for help. I had to often go for work in the nights and my wife would feel very lonely those times. During the first year of marriage, since either her parents or my parents would come visiting us, she did not feel very lonely or homesick often.

The birthday of my wife, her first after our marriage, soon approached. I wanted to give her a nice gift and asked what she desired. I expected her to say that she wants a bottle of perfume or ornaments or clothes. She said that nothing would please her more than having a nice Labrador pup as a gift.

It was like a stinger missile blown on me. I tried to duck, but there was no way. I tried to reason out with her saying that I am in a transferable job and every two years' time, we need to shift homes and taking our dog with us would be a big hassle. Besides, a dog needs non-vegetarian food and for me cooking non-vegetarian at home is unthinkable. She replied that a dog can survive on *dal* and *rotis* and my other arguments held no water.

I changed track and said that it is very tough to toilet train a pup and our house would become dirty too often. She said she would take care of that. I said the dog would bark in the night and we have to spend sleepless nights. She said "most of the nights you are away on work."

I said that our dog would bite whoever comes home. She replied that she will train him to be sociable. Her final statement was that only by having a dog in the family, would I overcome my fear of dogs. She said "You are policeman and you know the worth of dogs. And your department has very nice dog squads everywhere. Being a cop, if people come to know that you are scared of dogs everyone will laugh at you."

This was too much to stomach. I decided then and there to live with both my wife and dog. On her birthday, her face lit up when she saw a black cocker-spaniel pup. Ever since, dogs have become a part of our home.

27

Be an Assamese

With my extended family, which included my parents-in-law, I had reached Guwahati in the night and had checked into a lovely guest house. Getting up early from bed, we were sitting on the sprawling lush lawns and enjoying the invigorating morning air looking at the mighty Brahmaputra. Pots of freshly brewed Assamese tea were placed for our consumption. Three varieties of tea were available and I was quite excited to taste the exquisite teas of Assam.

When the bearer started pouring tea into my father-in-law's cup, he refused point blank and asked for coffee. My wife said, "Dad, we are in Assam which is famous for tea. You won't get coffee here". "Dear, in the past 65 years or so never have I started my day without coffee. I just don't like tea, however good it might be. I want coffee and nothing else", he said. I butted to say that it is virtually impossible to get coffee in Guwahati. He said he would rather go without coffee than drink the light tea which I was so much enjoying. We were to stay in the North East for at least five days and how could we allow the old man to miss his daily doses of coffee seemed to be the thought my wife was having. She looked at me pleadingly.

I finished my tea and went out in search of coffee with a thermos slung around my shoulder. At that part of the day not a single café was open. Wayside *Dhabas'* had not heard of coffee. I went round and round the town and my driver kept pointing out at all the famous landmarks of Guwahati. After two hours of search, I located a departmental store which had instant coffee. I bought a big jar and returned to the guest house.

When I reached back, it was breakfast time and the family was around the dining table. I joined them triumphantly producing the jar of instant coffee. My Father-in-law said, "Son, you have missed noticing something". I gave a quizzical look. He pointed at his cup. He was drinking Assamese tea! I was stunned.

He said, "Your wife gave a long lecture and asked me to be a Roman while at Rome. So I thought I will give Assam tea a try. It really tastes good". Pointing at the coffee jar, I looked at my wife. She said, "We will keep it, I don't know when the old man will change his mind". I muttered a curse and sat for breakfast.

28

Last Ride Together

'Since we are selling our car tomorrow, let us take one last ride and go for dinner at a Five Star hotel' said my wife. "Why are your selling this old faithful after keeping it for so long?" queried my daughter. "Because I cannot afford to get it repaired again and again, and having become old I don't have the stamina to push it. Besides, I am getting a good price for it," I said. "Papa, Paddy (the nickname of our car Premier Padmini) has been with us through thick and thin. Since we hardly use it these days, there is no occasion for you to push it. Please remember, it is I who push the car when it stalls on the road and not you," retorted my son.

My wife intervened to say, "I have had enough of this car which has caused me lot of embarrassment. Don't you remember the day Lalita stopped and offered a lift to us in her Esteem when Paddy had stopped at Cubbon Park? I cannot forget the shame I experienced that day. Itis better we sell Paddy forthwith and buy a Santro car tomorrow." "Mama, you should remember that a car is a mechanical device and even a Mercedes can develop trouble," reasoned my son. "I am not interested in all that. I have decided not to sit in this car from tomorrow," asserted my wife.

When the six of us squeezed into the car, my daughter said "Look mama! Our entire family can fit into Paddy. In Santro not more than four can sit." My son asked "Papa! If you are disposing of Paddy because it is old then how you would feel if I send you to an old age home when you cross seventy?" I got annoyed and said, "Look, Paddy being 20 years old has outlived its utility. We cannot be sentimental about these things. And listen! I don't expect you to look after me when I am 70." At this outburst, as everyone became silent, my thoughts ran to the day I bought Paddy.

As a Junior officer on deputation in Delhi, I was not entitled to an office car. Having been used to a vehicle since joining service, this lack of transport created untold misery, especially because Delhi is a city of distances.

"How can you commute standing in over-crowded DTC buses? It does not befit your status," a refrain I often heard prompted me to buy a second hand car to serve me during my tenure at Delhi.

Driving in Delhi was tough. In the very first week, at a road junction the car in front of me suddenly braked resulting in a collision. The driver of the car in front got down, assessed his damage and saying "It's okay, it happens all the time in Delhi" drove away. A few days later, a Maruti car banged my car at the back. My wife got down, and noticing the deep dent Paddy suffered, went to quarrel with the culprit. Seeing a burly sardarji in the Maruti staring her menacingly, she returned saying. "It's okay, it happens all the time in Delhi!"

By the time I completed my tenure at Delhi, our Paddy had been dented on all sides. When we tried to sell it, the offers were so low that we decided to keep it with us for sentimental reasons. Naturally in Karnataka, our car was used very sparingly, either to take children to their tuitions or for our weekend trips. Because of disuse and old age, the car started giving trouble and it so happened that whenever I took it out, it would develop some snag or the other and soon it became only a show piece.

This and the taunts from friends, made me decide to buy a new car and negotiate for the sale of our Paddy.

When we returned home my son said, "Dad, did you not miss something? Our paddy did not give us a single problem during both the journeys?" "Yes son, I did notice it," I said, "we are then keeping the car back" said my daughter. "Look children, the rules of nature are that old order has to change giving place to new. Paddy will go tomorrow though our last drive was trouble free."

Saying this I kissed paddy goodbye. I could see tears in my wife's eyes.

29

(Imaginary) Lunch with Musharraf

When I received a message from the Indian Chief of Protocol that Gen. Parvez Musharraf desires to have lunch at my house, I was astonished. I was not a Delhi born like the General nor was I Lucknowi, like his charming wife. "Why was I chosen for this honour?", I asked the Protocol Chief. "Sir, the General is visiting Bangalore and wants to have home cooked food during his visit and since you are the only one to be security vetted by the ISI, you are the chosen one," said the chap from Delhi. I looked at my wife. She was excited and nudged me to agree.

"Mr. Chief of Protocol! we are delighted to host the General. I know they liked *Mulligatawny* soup and *Lentil 'Gosht'* when our PM gave a banquet in their honour. By the way, my wife is famous for cooking these items. But

Chief! I agree to your request with two conditions. Firstly, no security personnel should enter our kitchen to taste or check the food being served as my wife cannot cook when someone is breathing down her neck. And secondly, the General should not have tea with my neighbour and sworn enemy *Huriyatappa* who is anti-India", I said.

The Protocol Chief thought for a minute and said he would get back to me in an hour. My wife said "Our neighbour *Huriyatappa* is from the same college as the General. The General will never agree to one of your conditions and we will miss that golden opportunity forever". I did not react. However, fifteen minutes later, the phone rang conveying the General's acceptance of both our conditions.

The D-Day dawned. At 12 noon sharp the General arrived with his *mem saab.* When they praised the Mulligatawny soup, we had to remind him that *molaga tanni* was in fact, a South Indian creation! Later, when the couple was escorted to the dining table my wife said "General, we are basically rice eaters like some of you in Pakistan. I know you, liked 'Lentil Gosht' served to you in Delhi. I have also prepared 'Lentil Gosht' today since it will go very well with Basmati rice. We hope you enjoy it."

The couple politely nodded. They were served steaming hot rice with "Lentil 'Gosht'". The couple had not one, but three helpings and didn't touch any other dish on the table. After the hearty meal both of them profusely thanked my wife for the delightfully delicious 'Lentil Gosht'.

My wife, not able to hide her happiness, said "Mr. President, the 'Gosht' is our home product. We got only a dozen this year. Now a day, rearing it is a Herculean task as we have to guard against thieves who are all the time on the lookout for tasty things". The generous General's wife gave some more compliments about their tenderness of the 'Gosht' and invited us to visit them in Pakistan.

When it was time for farewell, my wife in true Muslim style brought a tray which was covered in a red velvet cloth and said "Maam, in honour of your visit to our humble abode, I want to present you with the main ingredient of the recipe you just enjoyed so much". Madam looked very pleased.

With a flourish, my wife opened the cloth and there sitting on the tray was a green Jack-fruit! The General raised an eyebrow. I said "your honour, what you ate sometime ago as Lentil 'Gosht' is nothing but South Indian Sambar. But since we are vegetarians, we substituted meat with raw jackfruit which is known as "Brahmin's mutton". Thanks for liking this vegetarian delight".

The General gave a meaningful look at Madam Sheba and departed.

I turned to my wife. She was fast asleep.

30

An 'Indian' Wedding

When my nephew Ramu suddenly announced that he is going to marry his colleague Sushma, the first question my sister shot was to which caste Sushma belongs to. Ramu said, "Amma, she is from our own community but she is a Hindi speaking girl from UP". My sister was disappointed to have her only daughter-in-law a non-Kannadiga, but didn't articulate it.

My brother-in-law was very firm that the wedding should be held as per south Indian customs. Sushma's parents wanted traditional north Indian wedding to be held at their home in Noida. The consensus was that the wedding would be held at the bride's place in both north and south Indian styles and transport and accommodation for groom's party from Bangalore would be met by the bride's father. Christmas day was fixed as the wedding date.

Our family priest, who was unable to accompany us, arranged for a priest at Delhi to officiate as the *'Purohit'* (priest)for the wedding. Many of our close relatives backed out of the trip at last minute even though my sister had offered a trip to Haridwar and Rishikesh as a bait. We blamed the north Indian harsh winter for their decision.

The moment we arrived at Delhi railway station, we were welcomed by the bride's relatives who had arranged a bus to take us to Noida. Since the *'muhurtham'* was fixed at 5.30 am the next morning, the Delhi *purohit* also joined us at the station. A gusty chill wind made us uncomfortable. Our escort distributed *'kambals'* thoughtfully brought by him. As we reached our hotel, we were told that the *'Mehendi'* will begin at 4 pm and the marriage will be solemnized at 10 pm.

Though we all were very tired, we reached the bride's home in time. The events that unfolded, made us feel as though we are part of the movie *'Hum Aapke Hai Kaun'*. Invitees started arriving by 9 pm. A clandestine bar set up at the venue by the bride's folks, became the most sought after place for most guests.

Even by midnight, the reception had not concluded and the guests who wished the couple were enjoying the king of good times. Feeling tired, my brother-in-law asked his *'sambandhi'* to order 'pack up' so that all of us could be ready for the early morning *muhurtam* as per our customs.

We hit out beds at 1 am. When my wife and I came to the hotel lobby at 4.30 am, except the groom and his parents, none of our relatives were to be found. We reached Sushma's house at 5 am. A sleepy servant opened the door. Our priest made hurried arrangements. Even at six, there was no sign of the bride or her folks. At seven, Sushma's mother appeared and said that it will take at least two hours for them to get ready. My sister looked at the priest. He consulted his books and said that the next *Muhurtam* is only after two months. My brother-in-law's face fell. I said "Do not worry, the wedding is already over". In north Indian style", retorted my sister.

31

Unholy Water

When my parents telephoned to say that they would be visiting us for a fortnight to spend time with their grandchildren, we were filled with joy. We were then living in a north Indian town and any visit from near and dear ones was welcome. We immediately started planning how to make their trip enjoyable, and decided that since mom was highly religious and God-fearing, she should be taken to famous temples located nearby.

First in my list was one of the 'Jyotirlinga' temples. Though we were tired after a hectic overnight journey, mother was overwhelmed seeing the ancient temple and was excited to fulfill her vow. After freshening up, we went to the temple straightaway. By the time, the *poojas* were done, it was almost noon. Having skipped our breakfast, we were hungry. As soon as we came out of the temple, our escort said that there is another temple nearby which should not be missed. Though I was reluctant, my mother insisted and thus, we visited this temple. The temple was located on a steep hill and we climbed up panting and puffing. The temple was inside a small dark cave and the only lighting there was a brass lamp. As we entered the temple, the priest who was smoking a beedi, asked us whether we have brought any offering. We said no, but dangled a hundred rupee note. He performed *'aarthi'* and gave *theertha* (holy water) in a table spoon. As usual my mother consumed it thrice and soon she started coughing. The holy water was pungent and foul tasting. Making faces, we trooped out.

I was curious to know the contents of the *theertha*. Despite the family opposition, I entered the temple again but lonely I had to. This time, the priest asked me whether I have brought a *'pahwa'*. I did not understand what he meant and asked him to explain. He showed me a quarter bottle of arrack. I got angry and asked him how dare, he demand liquor that too in a holy place. He laughed and said that the deity is fond of liquor and it is the only offering, the Lord accepts. So saying, he placed an arrack bottle to the mouth of the deity. Half the bottle vanished in one go. I was amused. I asked the priest to explain but he said one should not seek explanation of divine powers. In the pretext of perambulating the deity, I went behind it and saw a big vessel kept at its back. Whatever liquor that was poured in the mouth of the deity would collect in the vessel and a portion of the same was distributed as *'theertha'* and the remaining was probably consumed by the priest!

Elated over this discovery, I climbed down. My family members were hovering around my mother looking worried. She had swooned. It did not take me long to find out that the country liquor had its effect on the empty stomach of the staunch devotee!

32

Rome Wasn't Built in a Day

Believing in the adage, "Be a roman while at Rome", wherever I travel I try to live as a local enjoying visits to museums and monuments, savouring the local food and generally getting the feel of the place. When I got a chance to visit Rome with my wife, I wanted to make the best of it, since I had only a day to spend there.

As we were having dinner, my host said that the most important places in Rome are located in close proximity to each other and it is fun to see Rome walking. I jumped at his suggestion and bravely told him we will conquer Rome by foot in a day! Though my wife protested muttering that I am prone to the foot-in-the-mouth syndrome, I placated her saying we could take a cab if our legs gave way. The next morning, our host dropped us at a central point, handed me a tourist map on which he had painstakingly marked the important places and routes to be taken and drove away.

Our first place of visit was Trevi fountain. We marvelled at its magnificence, threw coins into it like others, spent some time there and walked to see the other famous fountains, Navona and Fontano Del Moro. The map indicated Spanish steps as a nearby landmark. By the time we went there we were hungry. Our hostess had packed *bisibelebath* and curd rice and we ate them with great relish sitting on the historic steps. Refreshed, we started walking again, and arrived at Roman forum containing the oldest and most important structures of the ancient city. "This place looks like Hampi", my wife exclaimed. I nodded. Exploration of the Forum, like Hampi, was quite exhausting.

After a while my wife said that she was tired and could not walk further. I told her we can at least see all the important land marks of Rome marked out by our Host and cajoled her to continue the walk and took her to the nearby Colosseum. She was quite tired, but my act of getting dressed as a Gladiator and taking photographs cheered her. It was tea time and we had some refreshments and gave rest to our weary legs. After tea, my wife wanted to return, but I told her that we don't come to Rome every day and must see, all we could see in a day. Slowly, we walked towards Piazza Del Poppolo, which I remembered seeing in an English movie. My wife complained of blisters on her foot and refused to move further. I made her sit on a bench and explored the surroundings alone.

By this time, the sun was setting. We had to cover some more landmarks. But my legs were also aching. When I tried to motivate my wife to visit at least two more sights before we called it a day, she firmly put her weary foot down. I told her that she should "be a Roman while in Rome". She retorted saying "Rome was not built in a day and cannot be walked in a day". Disappointed, we returned to our Host's home.

Note: *Bisibele Bhat* is a rice delicacy special to Karnataka

33

Mayor's Dinner

An international workshop took me to an African country a few years ago. The day the weeklong event began, we received invitations to attend a dinner hosted in our honour by the City Mayor the same evening. Our joy knew no bounds. During our sojourn abroad we were entitled to get an allowance of 25 dollars daily for incidental expenses. Since we stayed in a bed and breakfast hotel and since our lunch and tea were to be provided by the organisers of the workshop, twenty five dollars were sufficient for our dinner and sundry expenses. But like so many of our colleagues, we wanted to save some dollars for buying some small *'phoren'* articles for our family members. Any opportunity which afforded even ten dollar savings per day was welcome.

Hence the mayor's invitation was greeted with cheers by my friends.

Nicely with duly trimmed bodies, we arrived at the ocean side resort exactly at the appointed time. There were a number of sign boards directing us to the dinner venue. When we followed the signs, we found ourselves facing a big welcome arch. As we were about to enter, someone shouted 'STOP'. We thought our invitations would be checked and took them out from our pockets. A group of about twenty Africans dressed in tiger skins suddenly jumped in front of us. Some of them started beating drums and the others who had painted their faces and bodies danced rhythmically to the beat. After five minutes, the dance stopped. The group leader then came forward, shook our hands and said that they had given us a traditional welcome. We proceeded further.

There was one more welcome arch to cross. Here stood the City Mayor wearing a chocolate coloured robe. He was also wearing a huge necklace of medallions. As he pumped our hands, my friend Sharma nudged me. Two young women were leading a pair of cheetahs inside the venue. The Mayor observed that we were apprehensive. "Friends, don't get scared. They are tamed cats brought here for your entertainment", he said. As if to second him, one lady asked Sharma to pat the Cheetah she led. Sharma reluctantly did so. The Cheetah didn't growl. We took a photograph and went inside. There was lot of music and dance. We parked ourselves at a table. Soon a bearer came with a choice of alcoholic drinks. Our colleague Verma asked for wine, Sharma took a beer while I opted for Scotch. There was a variety of snacks which we tucked in hungrily. We were happy that we had saved 25 dollars that night. Getting free booze in the bargain was indeed a bonanza.

Precisely at 12 midnight, the party ended. As we got up from the table, a waiter came to me and presented a piece of paper. I looked at him quizzically. He said "The bill Sir!" I took out my specs and read the paper properly. I had been billed Twenty Five pounds for four measures of Scotch whisky. Naturally I got annoyed, "Look gentleman! we are the guests of your Mayor. You cannot demand money from us. This is after all, a reception given in our honour. Presenting a bill for our drinks amounts to insult." He said that while he did not present a bill to my colleagues it was only I who was required to pay. Confused, I knitted my eyebrows. He said, "Sir, your friends had beer and wine which are not spirits. You consumed spirits and we are charging everyone who drank whisky or brandy or rum." All my colleagues gave out a loud hysteric laugh.

With a great sense of frustration and loss, I reluctantly paid the entire amount and quickly went out of the venue planning how to make good the loss in the next few days.

34

Nature's Call

Having been a canine lover only after my marriage, I am awed by the Europeans' love for their dogs. I was surprised to see during a recent visit that in most public transport, dogs travel free. They have designated places to sit and there are hooks where their leashes can be tied. It was amusing to see that when two dogs are travelling in the same bus, they don't snap or bark at each other. They silently growl and travel peacefully. The dogs don't even acknowledge the presence of other human beings! In fact, in a tram when a small dog, silently sitting on the floor, was about to be trampled by a passenger, it was only the dog handler who gave a warning. The dog was silent.

While admiring the behaviour of dogs in Europe, I kept thinking how the canines would ease themselves in public. I had read somewhere that even the best behaved dogs cannot resist peeing on the wheel of a parked car. The Europeans seemed to have a solution. I saw a circular enclosure in a public park with a pole at its centre. Affixed to the pole was a symbol of a dog urinating. The dog handlers were supposed to lead their dogs to the central pole, where the urine smell of others would induce the dog to urinate.

But how to make the dogs clear their bowels in an earmarked place was my next doubt. In the US, I had seen dog handlers carrying a bag and a scoop to take away the excreta of their wards. I had not seen this in Europe. When I saw signs on the footpaths warning dog owners that dog excreta on the footpath would cost 65 euros, I thought that it is impossible to make the dogs pass their stools at an earmarked place.

As a former cop, I kept thinking as to how the authorities could collect the fines from the culprits. I imagined that even if cameras recorded which dog relieved itself in which place, how could the owner be located to pay the fine? I got an answer soon. While on a morning walk in a park, I saw an old lady with two dogs. As they crossed me I saw both the dogs wanted to relieve themselves and despite all her might, the lady could not pull them away and the dogs happily attended to the 'nature's call'. The lady gave me an embarrassed look. I muttered that after all dogs are dogs, cameras notwithstanding.

A few days later, after taking photographs of the famous 'Mannekin Pis' monument in Brussels, I was walking along. My wife pointed at two lovely Labradors walking ahead of us.

My trained police eye easily spotted an oddity. Both the dogs were wearing a garment. I had seen dogs wearing woollens to fight the cold, but what I had not seen was a dog wearing underpants. Yes, both the black dogs were wearing black underpants.

While I could not fathom the reason for the dog owner to make his dogs wear underpants, my son remarked, instead of paying a fine of 65 euros - aren't underpants cheaper? My wife said, "May be to prevent the dogs being influenced by the famous monument". Till date, I haven't fathomed the reason.

35

My Day at the Races

Except for surreptitiously watching horse races from my class room window at college (which was abutted to Bangalore Turf Club), I had not actually gone inside a race course either to bet or to simply watch the horses run. One evening, when my friend Sharma suddenly appeared in my office and thrust an invitation from the Turf Club to witness the races, I was confused. The Chairman had invited me along with wife to witness the Chamundi Cup and to partake lunch and tea. A dress code was also prescribed. Since I am most uncomfortable wearing a suit, my decision was instant, I declined.

Sharma is not a person to take no as an answer. He explained how difficult it is to become a member of the Turf Club whose elections are tougher than parliamentary polls and how by sheer good luck, he had got its membership. "Guru! this is an hour of glory for me and you are my first guest as a club member. If you don't come, our friendship of quarter century will end," - he threatened. I was cornered.

When I went home and told my wife that I am taking her to witness horse races, she became livid. My explanations fell on deaf ears and she refused to accompany me.

The next day, I ferreted out my dark suit, pressed it and got into it. My children gave one long look at me and burst out laughing. My wife also joined them, and said, "Dear, this is your wedding suit which my dad presented you two decades ago. Over the years due to laziness and booze, you have outgrown it." I quickly got out of it and decided to stay back. My son read the invitation and discovered that one could wear a Safari suit too. I wore my best safari and breezed out.

Sharmaji who was at the club entrance, was disappointed that I didn't bring *Bhabi* along. I murmured an excuse and went with him to the second floor. He led me to a chair, introduced me to his friend Suresh, thrust a mug of beer in my hand and vanished. Suresh at once made out that it was my first day at the races. Soon the first race began, I looked at the horses and said No.3 will win. Suresh looked at a booklet, gave a wry smile and said, "Sir! Horse No. 3,Lady Love has absolutely no chance." Within fifty seconds, Lady Love had won! Suresh looked at me admiringly and asked, "Are you an astrologer?" He quickly went out and returned along with a boy and two mugs of beer. He asked me to place a bet with the boy. I said that I have resolved not to gamble. He said, "Sir! you needn't gamble with your money. I will finance your bets. If you win you give me fifty percent of your winning and if you lose, you give me nothing". I agreed.

When I selected the winning horses for the next two races, Suresh placed bets for both of us. Surprisingly, both horses won. Suresh placed two five hundred rupee notes in my hands being my share. In the meanwhile, Sharma came and pulled me for lunch. When Suresh told him about my prowess, Sharma said that it is only beginner's luck. I too agreed. We had a hearty lunch and immediately, thereafter I begged leave as I was too sleepy after the beer and heavy lunch. But Suresh would not let me go. He pleaded with me to stay till tea and predict the *trinella*. When Sharma also joined him, I reluctantly agreed and we went back to our seats. Suresh called the boy, purchased some tickets and bet. I surmised that if I also bet the money which I had already won along with the money which Suresh was giving me to play, I could actually earn a lot, I placed my bets.

In the first two races of the Trinella, the horses which I had predicted romped home victorious. There was only one race to go and there was a rush of adrenaline in me. I had picked up Queen of Sheba, which incidentally was also the favourite. The races started. In the first and the second bend, Queen of Sheba was leading the pack. Suresh held my hand tight and said, "Sir, soon we will win good money". In the last leg Queen of Queens almost came abreast and both the horses finished neck to neck. Sharmaji said that we have to wait for photo finish result. Out of nervousness, I started chewing my nail. At last, the results were out. Queen of Sheba was declared the winner. We were overjoyed.

Suresh went to the counter and brought a bundle of notes and placed Rs. 25,000/- in my hands. I placed them carefully in my pocket and went home. When my wife opened the door, I gave her all the money. She quizzed me like an Inspector in crime branch. When she was convinced that the money was actually my winning from the races, she asked me "Why don't you also become a member of the Turf Club like Sharma?".

36

Exchange Mela: Buy New, Give Old

"Dear, did you see this ad in the *Deccan Herald*?" asked my wife, her shrill tone becoming shriller. Knowing that she gets excited seeing advertisements offering freebies, I kept mum and continued reading. "I don't know that your hearing is already impaired. Sure sign of getting older," she taunted. I didn't lift my head. "Mr. Old Man! this ad helps you save a lot of money," said she.

I knew she had targeted my big weakness. Savings has always been my weakness and I would go any length to save that one last rupee. Throwing the newspaper away, I replied, "Okay! tell me, what new saving scheme has been launched?"

"No sir, this is not some *Bachat Yojana* of the Government. This is purely a private endeavour," she said. "Do you know how much money we get for selling old clothes, knick knacks, used bottles and other junk?"

"That is definitely your area of specialization my Dear, I know for certain that you exchange all our old clothes for steel utensils. I really don't know how much a kilo of junk costs. What I know certainly is that the cost depends on the opportunity" I said.

She gave a knowing smile and said, "Dear Hubby, this ad is from a Bargain Store. They are buying old papers, books and magazines at Rs.10 per kilo and old clothes at Rs.25 per kilo and other items at Rs.7 a kilo. It is three times the market rate."

"What is the catch?" I asked.

"You have to purchase from their shop goods equivalent to the amount of junk purchased by them." She replied.

I said, "This is what is called a fair deal. It is like any *Exchange Mela*. Let's go!"

During the next five hours, we sifted through all our loved belongings. We set aside books, bags, newspapers, old shoes, chappals, aluminum utensils and brass bowls which had been gifted to me every time I got transferred while in service. Soon we could fill five full sacks of junk. We had over a quintal of assorted waste. We would get more than Rs. 2000.

All five sacks went into my old Fiat car. The store assistant weighed each item separately and wrote Rs.2300 on a slip of paper. I was full of joy and felt as though I had hit the jackpot. After weighing the junk the clerk said, "Sir, you are entitled to get Rs.2300 off on any item purchased in this shop, but to avail this benefit, you must buy items worth five times this amount." He explained that we were supposed to buy items worth Rs.11,500 and on that amount, we would get Rs.2300 off. Though poor in arithmetic, I quickly calculated that I needed to spend over Rs.8000 to dispose of five sacks of assorted junk I had.

I looked at my wife. Without uttering a word, she patiently started putting back all the junk into the sacks.

37

Bitter Dharwad Pedas

After attending a marriage in a distant place, my wife and I were returning home. Having already travelled for more than six hours, we were quite tired and when the bus stopped at Hubli, all we wanted was to have some refreshments and sleep as the onwards journey to Bangalore was over-night. Many of our co-passengers left the bus to have their dinner in nearby eating joints. I told my wife that since Hubli bus stand is notorious for suitcase lifters, we should have some snacks in the bus itself. As we were eating snacks, a person selling '*Ilkal* sarees' entered the bus and approached us asking whether we would like to buy one. I was wary of traveling salesmen and disapproved of any transaction with them. My wife said that the sarees being sold looked like genuine *Ilkal* silk and such sarees in Bangalore would cost more than Rs.2000 each. Since the salesman is selling it for Rs.500, my wife felt that it was real silk and we should therefore, buy at least four. I gave her a dirty look. She winced and kept quiet. My lecture to her on cheats made her silently sulk.

A newly married couple was sitting next to us and the salesman approached them. Having overheard my wife's opinion, the young lady was eager to buy the sarees. The lady selected two of the six sarees, the salesman had with him and asked for two more with different designs. The salesman told her that his colleague had more sarees outside and that he would go out and return with them. He asked her to pay Rs.2000 and keep all the six sarees with her till he brought the other ones. She agreed. The salesman went out. Five minutes elapsed and there was no sign of the salesman. The couple got jittery. The husband went in search of the salesman and after a long search returned in vain.

By then, the bus driver returned from his dinner and started the bus. Passengers began trickling in. The newly married lady kept shouting that the bus should not proceed until the salesman was traced. However, the husband reasoned with her saying that as she had got six sarees for the price of four, she should not crib.

As they were arguing, some lady passengers approached the couple and began examining the sarees. After a thorough look over, they said that the sarees under examination were neither pure silk nor were made in *Ilkal*, and that similar sarees are available in the Hubli market for less than Rs.250 each.

I shot a smile in my wife's direction and boasted about how we had saved our hard earned money by discouraging the salesman. I claimed that I have never been in such awkward situations as I am very careful and not impulsive like her.

In the meanwhile, the conductor entered the bus and gave the signal for the bus to proceed. He was counting the passengers in the bus and the driver was slowly reversing the bus. Precisely at this time, one person selling 'Dharwad *Pedas*' came near our window. Being very fond of sweets, that too milk Pedas from Dharwad, I hailed him. The vendor said that the *Pedas* are from the Babu Singh Shop, which is very famous, and gave us a sample to eat. We both ate and found the sweet to be extremely tasty. We purchased six packets for ourselves and four more for our friends back home. As the bus started moving, we fell asleep.

After reaching home, in order to distribute the *Pedas* to our close relatives and friends, I opened the packets. Neatly placed in the packets were pieces of brick looking exactly like 'Dharwad *Pedas*'.

38

Senior Bureaucrat and the Common People's Party

The Senior Bureaucrat (SB) had just arrived at his office. Showing a newspaper his Personal Assistant (PA) said, "Did you see this news item Sir?" SB gave a quizzical look. "Sir, your junior in service has become a Chief Minister" "What if?" said the SB. "Sir, why don't you understand that while your junior is a CM, you continue to work under politicians. You are popular, you represent a strong community, are unofficial advisor of many CMs, past and present, trouble shooter for Ministers and alas! you are only a bureaucrat. All of us want to see you in a new role!"

When asked to be specific, the P.A. said, "Sir, you have just two years of Government service left. You have already reached the top and if you don't plunge into politics right now, you will retire unwept and unsung."

Precisely at that moment, the General Secretary of a National Political Party called the bureaucrat on the telephone and asked him to come to Delhi to sort out a ticklish problem, the party was facing. The beaming officer gulped one more cup of tea and asked his assistant to book his ticket to Delhi forthwith.

On his return from Delhi, the officer informed his assistant that the bosses of the National Party not only implemented his suggestions but also invited him to contest the next Parliamentary elections on the party symbol.

The assistant frowned and said, 'We want you to be Chief Minister of our State and not an MP who gets lost in Delhi.' A visibly annoyed officer said, 'you do not know politics, only if I become MP, can I stake a claim to be a CM, and in Politics one has to have lots of patience.'

'Sir! surveys show the Party which has invited you, has been losing popularity. Besides, many influential members of that party are against you since you insulted them a few years ago; they will work for your defeat. You should contest from the Common Peoples Party instead.'

The officer replied, 'Though I agree with you, I will not join CPP. They are all political novices. And the chief, who is my junior in service, dislikes me and refuse to give me a ticket to contest.'

The Assistant said, 'Sir! in politics, there are no permanent friends or enemies. Ability to win elections is what matters and you are the winning horse.'

'You are once again exhibiting your political ignorance. CPP can win in a small north Indian State and not in a big State like ours. In the next election, there will be a hung parliament and only the United People's Party which is now in opposition will play a crucial role and I have decided to join that party. You know the top leader of that party is my business associate.'

A few days later, the officer called his Assistant and announced that he will after all, join the Common People's party. "Sir! what happened?" queried the Assistant.

'The local leaders of that party have poisoned the minds of the High Command. I was told to wait till the next Assembly elections and cannot contest the forthcoming parliamentary elections.'

The Assistant clapped his hands and said, 'that is wonderful news Sir! now you have no other option but to join CPP. Shall I get the CM of CPP on the phone line? The officer nodded.

At that moment, a squad of anti-corruption bureau entered the room and announced that they have registered a case against the officer and will search his office.

The Assistant felt sorry that the doors of CPP, whose main plank is fighting corruption, were permanently closed to his boss.

39

The Day I Dyed

When I first noticed grey strands in my hair at the age of 35, I decided to ignore them. However, my colleague Harish Kumar from Haryana noticed the same and said that he had started graying at the age of 30, and has been successfully using henna to look youthful. Advising me to do the same, he brought me a kilo of henna from his village and told me that apart from making the grey strands turn brown, the green powder also has a soothing effect on the skull.

The very next day, I followed Harish's advice and found the grey stands in my hair turned dark brown. I was very happy with the result and continued applying henna for almost eight years.

When more and more black hairs started turning grey, the application of henna did not have the desired effect. My family members advised me to give up henna and to grey in a natural way. My daughter said, "Papa, you look dignified with grey hair." I bowed to their advice and discontinued applying henna to my hair.

However, whenever I saw my colleagues and classmates who were applying hair dyes, looking younger than me, one corner of my mind would urge me to apply hair dye. I fought all such urges, reminding myself constantly of harmful effects of the chemicals in the hair dyes.

One day, my mother chanced upon a new type of henna called 'black henna'. Presenting a few packets to me, she said, "Son, this is a new brand of henna and I am told it has no side effects." I was tempted to try it. In order to get the best effect, I grew my normally short hair, fairly long.

That day happened to be a Sunday. I opened the black henna packet, poured the entire contents into a bowl of water, applied the same on my head and had a nice bath. When I emerged out of my bathroom, our maid servant Lakshmi took one look at me and started laughing loudly. When my children saw me, they laughed even louder. On hearing the commotion, my wife, parents and servants came into the hall, saw me and started laughing in unison.

I was confused; I ran into my room and looked at myself in the mirror. My hair had turned jet black, blacker than the blackest charcoal. It looked as if I was wearing a brand new wig. My wife promptly brought a bowl of castor oil, and massaged it on my head vigourouly. She then asked me to wash off the oil first with *shikakai* and later with shampoo hoping that the black colour would vanish.I followed her advice scrupulously On coming out of the bath, I looked at the mirror. The colour remained. I applied gram powder on my head and tried to wash off the colour going to the bath room the second time. The colour was steadfast.

When I attended a family function later in the day, my relatives stared at me and asked me as to why I was wearing a wig! Totally embarrassed I returned home at once and went to my barber and asked him to do something.

Barber Babu asked me how it had happened. I explained. He took out a similar packet of black henna from his shelf and asked me whether it was the same brand I had used. I nodded. He said, "Sir, how much of this packet did you use?" I said I had used the entire packet. He said, "This packet is meant for ten applications and you have used the entire packet in one application." I grinned sheepishly and asked him to do something. He said the only solution is to shave off my head. I refused. He finally managed to give a very close haircut but I could not regain my original look.

For the next two days, I applied for leave and did not stir out of home. On the third day, I noticed that the top portion of my hair was black whereas the lower portion was turning grey, giving my face a very funny look. I could not avoid going to work, as I didn't have adequate leave. Though my friends and colleagues observed the change, they did not pass any comments. However, within the next fifteen days, I went to my barber again and had another haircut. My 'original' look came back.

Since then I have greyed gracefully.

40

Zest For Life

I spent a few months with my son in Ghent, a historical town in Belgium, soon after my retirement from Government Service. I was curious to see how people of my age live in Europe.

The thing that struck me most, was the extensive use of the bicycle in that town. Everyone from the age of five to seventy appeared to be riding bicycles. I was informed that cyclists have the right of way and they can ride as they please! I thought most cyclists consider themselves as the kings and queens of the road. My son asked me whether I too want a cycle to move around. When I politely refused stating that I have a knee problem, he took me to the local Transport office and got me a pass for unlimited travel in the Flemish Province. The moment I disclosed my age the clerk at the window said - as a senior citizen I am entitled for a discount of thirty per cent on the fare. He also added that had I been five more years older, I could travel free everywhere!

The first opportunity to use my pass came on a Saturday. As I sat in the bus, I noticed that most passengers who used the bus that day were cheerful looking senior citizens which made me wonder where they were headed to on a Saturday. I could gather later that the reason for their mass travel and cheer is that on weekends, they normally visit their children who live away from them and the Bus pass comes in handy.

To visit the Sunday market the next day, when I took a tram, it was also chock-o-bloc with of senior citizens. The men were in their best suits and the women in colourful dresses wearing high heeled shoes and faces fully made up. Some had their pet dogs too. I surmised that they were going to the church. But when all of them got down at a flower market, my curiosity got the better of me and I followed them. They all gathered at an open space. Soon a bagpiper came and started playing. The elders started humming and dancing. In the meanwhile someone setup a wine counter. The gents and ladies circulated among each other, enjoying themselves to the brim. Around noon, tables were laid and lunch was served. After their lunch, they bid adieus and dispersed. I learnt that these elders are the original inhabitants of the town and meet every week over lunch. The weekends definitely belong to the senior citizens, I thought. What impressed me was their enthusiasm to live life full.

The next weekend, I watched from my window five old ladies cycling on the road joking and laughing. Their little grandchildren less than ten year old were riding ahead. I remarked to my wife, "Look at these grannies, they cycle so well and are so fit at this age. You are not even fifty but constantly complain of knee pain and don't even climb stairs." She said, "Did you not see, the *nanis and daadis* are riding along with their granddaughters. Since everyone is used to cycling from a very young age, which keeps them fit even after sixty, they are not dependent on their kids like we in India. And did you not observe that they keep themselves busy, relish life and don't get tired after retirement both mentally and physically? Just because you have crossed sixty you have lost all zest for life and spend all your time reading newspapers or watching TV. I only hope that you will change when we return home"

That parting shot was really a learning point.

41

My Tryst with Customs Officials

It must be something to do with my face, or my gait, or my body language . As a former policeman I think it has to do with all the three. Whenever I try to pass through the green channel of customs in most western countries, I have invariably been stopped, asked to step aside and open my suitcases for inspection.

It must also be something to do with what I normally carry on my trips abroad. Being a *pucca* vegetarian and being addicted to having "curd rice" to end every meal, I have always made it a point to carry all essential food items we south Indians are used to consuming daily—*chutney* powders from both north and south Karnataka, *"gojju"* paste, assorted pickles, Andhra *gongura pachadi* etc. The quantity depends on the duration of my stay in the foreign land and the non-availability of Indian stores in the places of my stay. I also pack enough amounts of savouries like *Murukku, Kodubale,* Mixture and other short eats. However with the advent of MTR pre-cooked heat and eat foods, long stays in foreign countries have become more "palatable" and I carry less of eatables with me.

Due to strict security measures post 9/11, most of the foods I carry, except of course, *chakkulies* and *kodubales,* normally find their way into my checked in baggage.

A few years ago on my trip to Australia, as the plane was about to land, the video screens in the plane displayed a visual which informed that no food item is allowed in Australia and any passenger carrying such items, should throw them in the special garbage bins kept in the corridor leading to the customs lobby. It also warned that smuggling of any food item would result in imprisonment. The customs declaration forms had specific mention of this. I felt nervous as I had loads of short –eats in my hand baggage.

Since Australia's first inhabitants were prisoners from Britain, I imagined being imprisoned in jails like the ones I had seen in the Andamans. While I didn't want to consign the snacks , which my wife had so lovingly prepared , to the garbage bin in the airport, I didn't want to be confined in a Jail either. I resorted to the obvious. I opened my handbag and before the plane came to a halt on the apron, consumed the one week quota of Snacks and washed them down with a glass of water. I sailed through customs with a smile.

Six hours later I had to visit a doctor urgently, pay a hefty fee and get myself cured of the "after effects" of the short-eats. I resolved not to carry any food item to a foreign land and stopped taking eatables during my visits abroad.

However when I was to visit Israel recently, someone told me that plain yoghurt is not easily available there. Addicted as I am to curd rice, I hit upon an idea. I purchased a dozen tubs of probiotic yoghurt and kept them in my hand bag after specially sealing the containers. When I neared the customs green channel at Tel Aviv, a uniformed guy approached me. Being scared of Israeli Security, I started profusely sweating. The gentleman stared and asked me whether I am carrying any food item. I hesitantly said 'Yes' and proffered my bag. As he slowly opened the zipper the plastic bag carrying the yoghurt tubs caught his eye and he promptly began opening it. Suddenly, a muted sound akin to a minor explosion was heard. I became very nervous indeed. But when I saw the face of the customs officer, I could not suppress my laugh. His entire face was smeared with Yoghurt.

It was not difficult to guess that due to internal pressure, the seal of the yoghurt tub had popped open as the customs man opened the bag and its contents had sprayed his face. I offered to wipe his face with my 'hanky'. The menacing look he gave me made me run towards the exit.

Since then I have learnt to live without curd rice in an alien land.

Note: *Gojju* paste, and *Gongura Pachadi* are items one mixes with rice and eats. *Kodubale* , *Murukku* and *Chakkulies* are known as *Namkeen* in North India

42

Friday, the Thirteenth: Impact of Ritual Restriction

"Didn't you know today is Shasthi, a day forbidden for travel? Why did you buy air tickets for today's journey?" asked my 80 year old mother. I replied, "Staying a day extra in Mumbai would have cost a fortune. Besides I got a good deal for buying a group ticket". "Have you forgotten that you met with a serious accident when you and your wife travelled on a Shasthi day last year? I thought you would have become wiser after reaching 60, but you haven't changed a bit" - she said. I clenched my teeth but kept quiet.

As we reached the check in counter, the assistant saw our group ticket and muttered, "You're a group of thirteen, the youngest being one year old and the oldest eighty" and gave our boarding passes.

My son immediately remarked, " Grandma, did you notice the coincidence? Apart from being Shasthi, today happens to be Friday the 13th. We are thirteen in number. Many in the western countries wouldn't normally travel on such a day". Mother said, "Look even Westerners keep such beliefs, but your dad is so reckless he is making an entire family travel on an inauspicious day, I don't know what is in store for us". To tease my mother further, my son said, "ajji , dad would say that for safety reasons, PM and President of India won't travel in the same plane but he is making all of us fly together" I told my son to shut up and said, "Amma! nothing like that will happen. Do we have accidents each Shasthi day?" She turned her head away.

My mother was in a mood of gloom in the departure hall. Efforts by me and my children to lighten the mood went in vain. Soon we boarded the plane. As the plane was to take off, my daughter made the observation that it was 1 pm which in effect was 13.00 hours. I gave her a menacing stare.

While welcoming us, the air hostess said that the flight commander is from Columbia. My son reacted loudly, "Dad, I read in the papers most recent air crashes in India are due to lack of comprehension of Air Traffic control directions by non-English speaking pilots". My wife observed that Colombians speak Spanish. Mother asked us to beware of Astu gods, who make true whatever we say, and keep quiet.

An hour into flying, our aircraft hit air turbulence and started shaking like a leaf in a storm. My mother firmly clutched her seat rest and started reciting *Hanuman Chalisa* loudly. Fellow passengers joined the chorus. As the prayer ended, the plane entered clear skies and there was a collective sigh from the passengers which sounded like thunder.

We landed smoothly. As we came out of the aircraft a light drizzle started. My mother looked at heavens with both hands folded and said, "This is a good omen. Gods have pardoned you and saved our family. Never again embark on a journey on Shashti".

I said, "okay Amma, I hope you have no objection if I travel on Friday, the thirteenth".

"You have to be a Roman while at Rome", she said.

Note: *Shashti* is the sixth day of the Lunar fortnight. *Ajji* means grandmother in Kannada

43

How Hapless are Dogs in India

Such hapless creatures these dogs are. Nobody likes to be called by their name. When I thought that our MP Shotgun Sinha is an exception, he compares himself to an Elephant and says that, *"an elephant keeps walking as the dog keeps barking"*. I think it is mostly in Hindi heartland that dogs are sneered at. In almost all Hindi films, we come across the term "*Kameeney*" being used synonymously with a dog - *Kutta*. Again in Hindi films, we have seen villains being threatened that "He will die a dogs death - *kutte ki maut marega*". Does this relates to the practice of stoning a rabid dog to death, I wonder!

It is not only in Hindi films that dogs are abused at. Even in Kannada, we use the terms, "the heavens will not care if a dog barks" and *Nayi padu* (dogs fate). But Kannadigas are more tolerant to dogs. Long ago, when Pakistan and China declared a war with us, our Professor had named his dog "**Bhutto**". His neighbour went one step ahead and called his pet '**Paki**'. Another named his dog **Chow-en-Lai**. When asked the reason, they said that it is the only way they could protest against our enemies! This practice of naming dogs on people we don't like still continues. Otherwise, how can we explain dogs being named as Hitler, Churchill, Khrushev and Nero?

I have also wondered why we don't give our dogs Indian names - we hardly come across names like Gandhi, Nehru, Ashoka, Harshavardhan etc. However, some time back my friend who was in awe of Tippu Sultan named his Doberman "Tipu". Not to be outdone, his cousin named his German Shepherd, "Kempe Gowda". Fortunately, these names did not create any problem those days as people were more tolerant.

Invariably dogs get named on things the owner likes - I had a friend whose dog was named - 'Old Monk". Another had named his dog "Whisky". In fact Whisky is a very popular name all round the world. Naming dogs on ranks in the army, like Major, Captain, General, Brigadier is also common but I am yet to come across names like Air Marshal or Wing Commander though Admiral is common.

Many expressions and idioms in the English language are also not complimentary to the breed of dogs. When we have severe summers we say, 'Dog days of summer". When two people fight, we say they are fighting like cats and dogs. When a person spoils things, we call him 'dog in the manager'. When a person is overlooked, we say he is in the doghouse. When we see an incorrigible person, we say, no one can straighten a dog's tail. We also call our boss, the top dog. If the boss merely shouts but does not harm, we use the expression, a barking dog never bites. We also know the meaning of the expression, going to the dogs.

We always acknowledge the presence of dogs in our lives. But, very few recognize the qualities of man's best friend, Syndicate Bank being an exception having put a dog on its logo.

It definitely takes a dog's perseverance to change things related to man's best friends.

44

Nourishing the Soul

On a recent visit to the US, my son suggested we go to a temple. Though not a frequent temple goer, I agreed when assured that it would be a nice weekend outing. Parking our car at a far end, we walked up to the temple built on a hillock, in biting cold. Standing before the magnificent idol of Lord Balaji adorned in the finest of jewelry, I felt I was in Tirupati. The priest gave a fistful of almonds as *Prasadam* which triggered off my hunger pangs.

As we went into the next building, the aroma of *puliyogare* wafted through and my legs automatically dragged me to the temple canteen. The big dining area was full and a long queue had formed in front of the self-service counters. I was amazed at the array of south Indian delicacies on offer. A friend of my son who bumped into us suggested going in for *puliyogare, pongal and vada*. We dutifully obeyed him. He brought his parents to meet us and during lunch, we were told that they had come to the temple to look for a bride. When I expressed surprise, they informed me that the temple has seen many wedding engagements, marriages and also naming ceremonies. When I looked around, I saw many young girls wearing traditional Indian ware towing their mothers dressed in Kanjeevarams.

The food we ate was indeed divine! I was told that cost wise, it was very reasonable too. My daughter in law bought a number of items as take away saying; "*Appa!* you can enjoy this for the next two days" I nodded in agreement.

The very next weekend, I suggested that we go to the Balaji temple again. My son smiled and said that he would take me to another temple. This time we went to Sri Rama Temple. Sensing that my mind was more on food, I was led to the canteen at the basement. I met a volunteer, a Kannadiga who was serving food. She suggested that I should eat *Idli-Vada* and masala *dosa* which are the specialties there. Soon she joined us and told me that a lot of families visit the temple for the sole purpose of having their weekend brunch (combination of lunch and breakfast both) and the canteen is kept open till 3pm. She added that while the canteen in Balaji temple is like MTR, the one we were in was like Vidyarthi Bhavan! She also said that the temple runs music classes on weekends keeping our culture alive. She however agreed that more than the deity, it is the canteen that attracts visitors, both Indians and Americans.

There was only one more week left for us to get back to India. My wife wanted to eat *Chat*, and a friend suggested that we go to Swamynarayan Temple. The visit was exhilarating indeed. The canteen too didn't belie our expectations. We had *samosas, dhoklas, kachories* and different types of sweets.

As we were returning to Bengaluru, I remarked that never in my life have I visited so many temples in three weeks. My wife, retorted saying," it is because the temples nourished your belly more than your soul". I asked, "Don't we consider food as God?"

Note: *Idli, Vada, Dosa, Pongal, Puliyogare* are names of South Indian snacks. *Dhokla, Chat, Samosas* and *Kachori* are popular North/West Indian snacks. *Kanjeevaram* is a type of silk saree. MTR and Vidyarthi Bhavan are restaurants in Bangalore (Now Bengaluru) hugely popular for their snacks.

45

Vagaries of Vaccination

"Sir, I have good news for you! We are going to Africa on office work next month. Have you been vaccinated against yellow fever?" asked my colleague.

I replied in the negative. "Sir, without a certificate showing that you are vaccinated against yellow fever, you can't get your Visa", he said.

I countered saying that when I have visited Egypt and South Africa without the vaccination, why I should get one now.

"Since Western Africa is prone for infections, you must be vaccinated. It is for your own safety", he reasoned.

He took me to the Government facility where the vaccine is administered only once a week. There was a long queue of people. He pulled some strings and took me straight to the doctor. The doctor asked me the name of the country I am visiting. I blurted the name. He looked at a long list of countries and told me that I need to get oral polio vaccine (OPV) also, which I can get from any hospital in Bangalore (now Bengaluru).

While administering the yellow fever vaccine, the doctor told me that I should expect to get body ache and fever and if this happens, I must report to him. I nodded my head and came back.

Two days later my colleague took me to a Pediatrician for getting OPV. As I entered the doctor's chamber, she looked at me and asked, "Where is your grandchild?"

I told her that he is sleeping at home.

She growled, "Why are you wasting my time; bring your grandchild"

My colleague butted in and told her that it is I who needed to be given OPV. She said, "Never in my thirty year long career, have I given OPV to a senior citizen" and refused to administer the drops.

My colleague showed her the letter from the Embassy which mandated that Visa applicants be given OPV. At this time, another doctor entered and a discussion ensued between both the doctors.

The younger one said that OPV is given only to small kids and old hags like me should be given injectable polio vaccine. I asked him the difference.

He said that OPV contains live bacteria and there is one in a million chance of getting polio due to live bacteria, I must therefore take IPV. I agreed and asked to be given IPV. The senior pediatrician said that they have only OPV in stock.

I turned my back and started walking away. My colleague forced me to sit saying "No OPV, No Africa". He made me open my mouth and asked the doctor to administer the drops. I had a very funny taste in my mouth.

Ten days later, I developed severe body ache and low temperature. I feared that I have contracted either polio or yellow fever and was nervous. I rushed to my physician who reassured me that I have a simple viral fever and put me on anti-biotics. After recuperating at home for a week, I went to office.

My colleague greeted me to announce that our African trip is cancelled.

The funny taste of OPV still lingers in my mouth.

46

Grandpa's Joy: An Attachment at Rise

The D-Day to welcome the new family member had arrived. The obstetrician who examined my daughter declared that the birth has to be through Caesarean section. I was nervous. After an hour of anxiety, I was told I have become grandpa of a baby boy. While all other family members were thrilled to see the new bundle of joy, I went to see my daughter first. Only after ensuring her well-being, I met my grandson.

He was very fair and tall. They told that he was born under the same star and zodiac sign as I and we both were born on the same day of the week. That indeed made him special to me. As it is customary for a daughter to spend few months at her maternal home especially after delivering her first baby, my grandson arrived at our home straight from the Hospital. He would be asleep during the day and awake during nights. Hence, I couldn't have much interaction with him in the first month.

In the later months, his sleeping habits changed and he started recognizing faces. My daughter would go to the internet and check whether her son is reaching the prescribed milestones. Once when I mentioned that the baby is not turning his face to the source of sounds, my daughter was worried. For the next one week, I would bring the bell from the "*puja*" room to the nursery, stand at different places in the room and ring it. If the child did not turn at the direction of the sound, we would both get worried.

My daughter was also concerned that the child had not started turning or crawling on time. My mother and other elders were least worried about these so-called "misses". Instead, they accused us of being paranoid and not worldly-wise.

Soon the little one started uttering sounds, turning on his stomach and standing up. And also turning at the direction of the ringing bell! Each of these moments brought extreme joy and my wife would cook '*payasam*' to celebrate each event. She would not hesitate to remind me and my daughter for being impatient about the child's growth.

Meanwhile, I noticed a change in me. I would spend more time at home than in office. Having hated shopping all my life, I started enjoying going to shops that sell kids goodies and spending hours buying things for the little one. I would even stop reading newspapers to spend time with my grandson. He was now the focal point of our life.

The day for my daughter to go to her home arrived. I was reluctant to let go of my grandson. He had brought a new meaning to our being. When I told my daughter that I can't live without my grandson, she told me "*Appa*! when I was an infant, you were too busy with your work and even when I was admitted to hospital as an infant, you couldn't spend time with me. You missed all the pleasures of rearing your children. Now that you have time to spare, you experienced the moments that you had missed. That's why you are more possessive of your grandson than your daughter".

How true, I felt.

Note: *Payasam* is a sweet dish made of milk; it is known as *kheer* in North India

47

The Case of the Missing Footwear

All through my police career of thirty five years, I have supervised investigation of thousands of tough crimes, like dacoity murder, cheating and rape as also Shad personally investigated many theft and murder cases. I take pride at being a good detective and also never being a victim of theft. An incident, that happened soon after my retirement from police service, changed this.

My cousin had built a new house in the outskirts of Mysore and had invited us for the house warming function. We reached the venue and since Satyanarayan *pooja* was being performed inside, we had to leave our footwear outside and enter the premises. Reluctant to expose my new costly footwear to any criminal eye I hid them at a nook and went in.

A *shamiana* was erected in the vacant plot outside for serving lunch. When I came out of the house for lunch, I was shocked to find my footwear missing. My wife taunted that had they been kept along with others, they wouldn't have been stolen.

Meanwhile many guests expressed pity and surprise that the footwear of a former Policeman was stolen. This was like rubbing salt on the wound.

Someone said "Look, you must have detected many a difficult cases, can you not detect your own stolen footwear?" Others joined the chorus.

Soon I set out to work. Surmising that since the new house was far from the town, the job would not be an outside one, I first suspected the catering team. I interrogated the cook and the waiters in true police style but drew a blank. My attention next turned on the guests. The task was to find the "Hawk-eyed" guest who could locate and lift the hidden footwear. I asked the host whether any guest had left the premises after my arrival. The host replied in the negative and said that all guests are close relatives and friends. My job became easy. As the first batch of guests sat for lunch, I went along with the waiters and gazed at the feet of each and every guest. Soon, I noticed my footwear adorning the feet of a decent looking gentleman. The host informed me that the gentleman in question, was his wife's uncle and a famous surgeon of Mysore.

A ticklish problem started at me. What if the surgeon refuses to acknowledge that the footwear is mine? What tantrum would he throw if he was caught? What embarrassment would this incident cause to the host? Carefully weighing all the pros and cons, I decided to get the case closed as "mistake of fact" as is normally done by the Police and buy a new pair of footwear.

My conscience, however, did not permit me to allow the stolen property being taken away in my very presence. I discussed the matter with my cousin's wife and sought her help. She asked me to wait till the surgeon would complete his lunch.

She invited the surgeon and his family inside her new home on the pretext of giving them return gifts. As the surgeon left my footwear and went inside, I rushed to the spot, wore my sandals quickly and triumphantly sat for lunch.

Later, I overheard the surgeon muttering that someone has stolen his footwear.

48

Brimming with Pride

We were transiting London airport on our journey to USA to be with our son for a few days. I saw an elderly Indian couple totally lost and worried. When I approached them to assist, I found that they didn't know any language other than Telugu. With my limited Telugu vocabulary, I could gather that they were from a remote village in AP and were travelling for the first time by air to visit their son in Chicago. With pride, they said that their son who has a" big job" in US had sent them air tickets. Since my destination was also Chicago, I asked them to join me and made them board the flight.

As I entered my son's apartment complex near Chicago, the smells that assailed my nose were that of Indian food. I was told that Indian techies have virtually taken over that residential complex ousting out other nationalities. Naturally on my morning walk, the next day, the people I came across were all Indians and the languages heard were Telugu, Hindi, Tamil and Kannada in that order. Many walkers of my generation would stop and greet me, enquire about me and my family, and would proudly inform me of their children causing annoyance to their children.

One Saturday, we went to a Balaji temple built through the munificence of Indian diaspora. It was as crowded as Tirupati temple. In the temple canteen, it was amusing to see youngsters showing the elders how to clean up their tables and put the used plates in garbage bins. Outside the temple, happy Indian families were getting their pictures clicked.

On a long weekend, we went to Niagara Falls and once there, I felt that I was back in India! Most visitors were three generations of Indians walking together. I didn't fail to notice the awe, fascination, pride and joy on the faces of visiting Indians. When we were relaxing on a park bench, a youngster brought along his mother and requested us to keep her company while he and his wife went sightseeing. The old lady proudly said that she lives in a small town near Pune having modest means. Her son, an Engineer, had bought a car and brought her sightseeing all the way from Washington DC.

On my return journey too, I met an Indian couple at the airport. They informed me that they run a small tailoring firm and made their son an Engineer making lots of sacrifices. Their son landed a job in an IT firm, got posted to USA and sends enough money home to take care of the family. They informed that while they have not even seen their state capital, they have seen US thanks to their son, who not only paid for their tickets but got them costly gifts.

I told them that their son is following true Indian values and definitely deserves appreciation, but our IT firms deserve a bigger thanks for bringing about a social revolution making even families at the bottom of the pyramid hold their heads high and proudly say that they are "foreign returned"

49

The Joy of HMT Watch

When I saw the school notice board declaring the tenth standard examination results, my joy knew no bounds.

For, I would now become a proud owner of an HMT watch as promised by my dad, since I had passed the examination in first class. I waited for my dad to come home and give me the promised gift.

He took me to the factory showroom located close to our home. I wanted only the 'most talked about' "pilot watch with the black dial" but alas, it was in short supply. The salesman asked me to buy another model but I was adamant about my choice. He said that we have to wait for a long time to get that watch, but if we knew someone in the factory, and lucky, we may get one. We came back home disappointed. Seeing my gloomy face, my mother persuaded my dad, who was in Government service, to pull some strings and get me the watch.

My sister remembers the happiness on my face when I saw that watch. From the very first day, it would remain on my wrist at least for twenty hours a day. To make others notice my watch, I started wearing it on my right wrist. I can never forget the admiring looks the watch and its wearer got from the girls in my college. Like the fashion in those days, I would roll up my collar in pride whenever such looks were received. Immediately thereafter, my friends would successfully persuade me to buy them a treat in the college canteen. After all, I was the proud owner of HMT Pilot watch!

The Pilot watch taught me great many a things early in life, and the most important was the value of time. I began to value not only my time but others too and this has made me manage time in a very efficient manner and achieve a lot.

The watch also taught me to respect swadeshi goods, to encourage and value products made in India. I felt a sense of pride wearing an Indian watch which was as good in looks or performance as a Swiss or a Japanese watch. On my return from trips abroad, I would amuse the customs men by flaunting my watch and say, "I am declaring this."

The HMT watch also helped me make many a new friend. Once on a tour to Srinagar, I noticed a signboard giving directions to HMT watch factory. Surprised to see my brand in Srinagar, I went to the factory on an impulse. As luck would have it, the manager of the factory was a Kannadiga and noticing my love for HMT watches, he took me home and gave me a typical Mysore meal.

A few years ago on a visit to USA, a person of Indian origin noticed my watch and came to me and introduced himself as a former employee of HMT watch factory.

During my two day stay there, he not only showed me all the important places around but also fed me home cooked food.

I am sad that HMT watch factory is taking a bow. With the launch of Apple Watches, I think it became inevitable. But the joy the HMT watches brought to millions of my generation can never be forgotten.

We all miss you HMT. Bye, Bye.

50

Mornings, a City's Mirror

While many people think that night life in a city indicates its vibrancy, it is the early morning life which gives a true picture of any human dwelling.

Pre dawn (*Brahma Muhurta*) is the time to know how people spend their nights. This is the time when night shift workers and party hoppers pack up and go home to have a good day's sleep. Once in Bangkok while briskly walking on the footpath, I heard loud music blaring from a parked vehicle. Seeing empty liquor bottles thrown on the pavement I guessed that a pavement party was still underway. Some partying sex workers present there accosted me and blocked my way asking me to utilize their services. With great difficulty, I could sneak out. In Cape Town, a bunch of drunk goons surrounded me to rob me but thanks to a police patrol car which appeared in the nick of time, I could get away to safety.

Pre-dawn, is also the time to see and smell freshly arrived vegetables, fruits and flowers. Any passerby in front of K.R.Market in Mysore will be exhilarated by the smell of Jasmine and sight of brinjals. Early birds in coastal towns can see freshly caught fish being sorted out and if lucky, buy the best catch at a reasonable price. Seeing the faces of satisfied fisher folks coming back home with a substantial catch is elevating.

Early mornings are also people's fitness time. One can come across people walking, jogging, doing yoga, clapping their hands. In Hanoi, I saw a group of elderly women convert a footpath into a gym and perform Chinese dance to the sound of blaring music.

This is also the time to see different breeds of pet dogs. I was amused to see walkers in New York carrying plastic bags and scoops to take away their pet dogs poop. I was surprised that people in Antwerp allow the dogs to spoil pavements despite seeing warning signs of hefty fines.

Mornings are times to know the breakfast habits. It is the time when roadside vendors do roaring business. In Saigon, one can see footpath vendors serving "pho", a soup with rice noodles, to customers sitting on low plastic stools. In Ghana it is Burgers and Sandwiches, whereas in Sri Lanka it is string hoppers with curry. While walking in the Little India area in Singapore the smell of fresh *Idlis* linger and while in Belgium it is the smell of Waffles and Potato Chips. The smell of filter coffee in Tamil Nadu makes one stop and sip from a brass tumbler. It is a sight to see busy office goers grab a plateful of breakfast on the streets and rush to their offices.

Dawns are also the time when the smells of printing ink wafts through. Road corners are full of Newspaper vendors.

As a media man once, I would learn which newspaper sells most in the town by talking to the vendors, apart from quickly glancing at all headlines. As the sun slowly rises, the air smells of Petrol and Diesel. The chirps of the birds recede and the city comes to life with lot of noise.

Mornings, wherever in the world, are a mirror to the lifestyle of the people who live there.

51

My Special GPS

As I started the car, my wife said, "I have told you a hundred times not to touch alcohol when you are driving, don't tell me that you were not warned if you get caught by the traffic cops". "Look! I had only one pint of beer and no alcometer would show me drunk", I replied. "You don't know your former colleagues, if there is a slight beep on the meter, they will book you and our tabloid tomorrow will scream 'ex-DGP booked for drunken driving'. You have suspended so many of them while in service. Do you think they will not take revenge?" she countered.

Silently, I put the car into gear. "How can you start the car in the 3rd gear? I have been begging you to hire a driver, but you are such a miser, you want to drive yourself". The car stalled and stopped. I got it moving and said, "My dear!

these days, you can get virtually anything, but not a driver for more than a week. Did we not have six drivers in the last two months? It is because of them, my car has deteriorated. Till recently, this car was as good as new". "Slow, slow, the lights are turning red" she said, and I slowed and moved on at the green signal.

"Brakes, brakes,"- she shouted. I obeyed instantly and the car once again stopped. I turned at her. "Madame! you are now beyond sixty. Not only me, but our children too are asking you to go to an optician and get your eyes tested. But you will listen to none, you are a stubborn person". "Madam! why don't you come to the point? Why did you ask me to apply brakes?"- I asked. "Did you not see that two wheeler suddenly come from the right and swerve to the left? We just avoided a collision. And if we had one, the headlines tomorrow would be, 'Drunken ex-DGP rams into a two wheeler'. Yes, that reminds me. Two days ago, there was a call from the insurers that this car's insurance has expired. Its really God's grace, nothing happened, otherwise we would be poorer by a few thousands. You are always penny wise and pound foolish. Could you not have checked up the expiry date and got insurance renewed?"

"Look dear! I am not driving above 30 kmph and there was no way that I would hit that speeding monster. By the way, I genuinely forgot the due date of the insurance". "Yes, how can you remember? All these past three and a half decades, you have been used to Secretaries and Assistants and orderlies who were taking care of these small things. Police Department has made you lazy and dependent. It is high time you start remembering that you have to stand on your own feet, now that you have retired from service"

On reaching home, my son who had just arrived from Europe innocently asked me whether my car has inbuilt GPS navigation. I pointed at his mother and told him that I don't need a GPS ever.

52

Age Cannot Wither Lady Countenance

As I boarded the wide bodied aircraft of our National Carrier, I noticed that the majority of the cabin crew was senior citizens like me and felt reassured that highly experienced crew will be taking care of my comfort during the three hour long journey.

The Senior Stewardess was a matronly lady, who I thought must have already clocked over a hundred thousand hours of air travel. Unlike others of her rank, she did not concentrate on business class passengers but decided to serve the *'aam janata'*.

When some passengers were finding it difficult to put their luggage in the overhead bin, the Senior Stewardess rushed to help them by sheer instinct. Alas, though the spirit was willing, the flesh was weak and while helping to lift rather a heavy suitcase I could notice her grimace. But she somehow accomplished the task.

As the flight cruised, the Senior Stewardess reappeared pushing a cart with snacks and beverages. The way she served each passenger with a smile was admirable. When it was the turn of my neighbour, our hostess realized that the non-vegetarian food that he wanted was exhausted. The passenger got angry and started shouting. Without losing her composure, the lady convinced him to eat the vegetarian adding an extra bowl of dessert as bonus. The passenger later muttered that it was exactly, the way his mother would act when some food was in short supply at home!

When half the passengers were dozing off after their meal, the silence was broken by the howl of an infant. A young cabin attendant came and tried to help the mother pacify the infant. The infant did not budge. Soon the Senior Stewardess arrived and carried and comforted the child. Within a few seconds the child stopped crying. The mother remarked that since the child is reminded of its grandmother, it felt comfortable and profusely thanked the Stewardess

I also noticed the Senior Stewardess correcting the mistakes of her young colleagues and helping them to learn the nuances of their job.

As we were approaching our destination the plane hit an air pocket and started wobbling like a dry leaf in a storm. On hearing the pilot's warning to be seated and fasten seat belts, all passengers, including most flight attendants, sat down. However, our Senior Stewardess did not sit down, but moved efficiently in the cabin asking people to fasten their belts and reassuring frightened passengers not to be anxious. In her zeal to help the passengers, she herself was tossed about and got hurt.

Undeterred, she smoothened her sari as though nothing had happened, and with a smile, she went to the nearest empty seat and tucked herself. She smilingly told the passengers that hers was a live example of what would happen if one did not sit and fasten seat belt during turbulences.

As the plane touched down and came near the terminal, many passengers got up from their seats and started opening the overhead bins. The Stewardess suddenly appeared on the scene and with a stern voice asked them to sit down as the seat belt sign was still on. Hearing her tone, many instantly obeyed her.

She was truly a leader, displaying many leadership qualities in the three hour journey. She never appeared fatigued and was a picture of composure. When I was leaving the aircraft and the lady said goodbye, I could not but compare the pretty young things that get recruited as cabin attendants nowadays with the graceful lady. After all, experience shows.

Thank you, National Carrier for respecting age.

53

Fascinating Chanakyapuri

Every time I visit the Diplomatic enclave in Delhi named after the great Indian Diplomat in Chandragupta Maurya's court, I learn something new.

As a school kid, I would gape at the colourful flags flying atop the embassy buildings and associate flags with their countries. I would also place each country on an imaginary world map and see how their embassies are located in Chanakyapuri. Neighbours US and Canada, Russia and Sweden are close to each other but not next to each other; Sweden and Finland being an exception. Similarly Afghanistan and Russia, are close in Chanakyapuri, even now, though literally Russia has gone hundreds of miles away. A walk in Chanakyapuri will indicate the new countries that have emerged in the world.

Like Czech Republic and Slovakia, (who have split the same compound), Uzbekistan and Bangladesh who are now away from Russia and Pakistan.

Driving on the majestic Shanti Path, my dad would tell me why we chose peace as India's mantra. I learnt about Non Aligned movement driving on Panchasheel Marg. Pointing at the main streets - Satya, Dharma, Niti, Nyaya and Vinaya, dad would exhort me to inculcate these principles which India believes in. As a young boy, I would also gape at the majestic Hotel Ashok, dreaming to stay in that Hotel one day and getting a lesson about Public-Private Sector.

As I grew older, I began appreciating the architectural marvels - the majestic US Embassy with its tall fountains, the blue domed Pakistan Embassy, the fort like Belgian Embassy, the wavy and uneven roofed Finnish Embassy, the hat shaped Singapore High Commission, the pagoda shaped Bhutan Embassy etc.

When I was in Delhi preparing for my civil services exam, I would invariably walk in Chanakyapuri and gather some tit-bits about various countries by looking at the huge notice boards in front of each embassy (those days there was no internet). I would see roads named after Gen Jose Artigas and Dr.Jose P Risal and learn that while the former was the father of Uruguayan Nationhood, the latter was a Filipino nationalist. Though I knew that Kwame Nkrumah was from Ghana, I came to know that San Martin was an Argentinian leader through a reference book. I knew about Andre Malraux, being a student of literature. My score in the General Knowledge paper definitely improved because of these walks.

After I joined service, I used to live in Karnataka Bhavan in Chanakyapuri. I couldn't but appreciate how various states in India also find a place in Chanakyapuri like various nations in the world. I feel that Chanakyapuri not only mirrors the wonder that is India, but the wonder that is our world. And just like those foreign countries our own states built lovely edifices, showcasing their strengths. And just like seeing Uzbek Embassy come up, I also witnessed Uttaranchal Bhavan coming up. And just as Sam Martin Marg, there is Bardoloi Marg celebrating our own Assamese leader Gopinath Bardoloi.

Now I am a Senior Citizen. And Chanakyapuri continues to fascinate and educate me and makes me feel inclusive.

54

Nectar-Drops of Human Kindness

It was past midnight when we returned to the city centre of Sydney after conclusion of our conducted tour. None of the taxis we hailed was willing to ferry us to our hotel stating that it is at a walking distance. Tired and sleepy, we started walking on the lonely footpath. My wife suddenly remembered that it was in Sydney that only a few weeks ago a Bengaluru girl had been killed and an Indian student was assaulted by a stranger the previous year. Though I reassured her that nothing like that would happen to us, I too was nervous.

As we were slowly trudging along, a taxi stopped next to us. The driver asked me where we were headed. I told him the name of the hotel and to my surprise, he asked us to board in. With great trepidation, we boarded the taxi and within a few minutes, we were in front of our hotel. When I opened my purse to pay the driver, he refused to accept the fare stating that we are the guests of Australia. When we insisted on paying, he said," I could make out that you both were very tired and seeing you I was reminded of my parents". While thanking him, I did feel a sense of guilt at having negative thoughts.

Cut to late 1984. When many parts of North India were reeling with anti- Sikh sentiments, I had embarked on a trip there with my wife and small kid. We had been to Kausani in Uttarakhand to see the sunset on the Himalayas. As we were about to leave for Almora, we were told that due to a landslide, the road was closed. Forced to spend a night in Kausani, we went from hotel to hotel, repeatedly to be told that there is no room.

Night had fallen. It was getting colder. My son was hungry and wailing. We were filled with panic. By accident, I saw a building with a sign board "Army Mess". My wife suggested that we look for a room there. I told her that the Mess is strictly meant for defence personnel and there is no point in trying. She did not take no for an answer and nudged me to take a chance. When we rang the bell, a burly Sardarji opened the door. I explained him the situation. He said that he is a caretaker and not authorized to allot rooms and moreover civilians cannot stay there. Our repeated entreaties made him relent and he gave us a room.

As we went inside, we noticed that we were the only occupants there and this caused us anxiety. We firmly bolted the door and hit the bed as we were tired. At about 10 pm, there was a knock on the door. With great trepidation, I opened the door to see the same Sardarji with a big tray. He placed the tray containing rice and hot sambar on the table saying, "Knowing that you are Madrasis, I asked a jawan to prepare food for you. Enjoy" he said and left that room. That was the tastiest Sambar, I have eaten.

I had realised in full the Quotation: The nectar drops of human kindness flows everywhere.

55

Are You Alive, Sir?

It was a month of intense depression for me since a number of my former colleagues in the police reached the lotus feet of the Almighty. It so happened that only those who had retired from Government service along with me or a few months earlier had been chosen by the Lord. After attending the funeral of one such soul, I went to see a comic play to come out of my gloom.

As I was laughing away to glory, my cell phone vibrated. I could easily identify the called party as the police control room of DGP's office. Out of sheer habit, I took the call. The caller after confirming that he is speaking to none other than myself asked me whether I am in a hospital. I said I came out of the hospital a few hours ago. He asked "Sir are you okay?" I said "I am perfectly alright". "Sir I am very sorry to be asked this question, were you admitted to the hospital?".

I was getting irritated since I had already missed a few laughs. My neighbour gave me a dirty look and asked me to go out of the hall if the call was so important. Meanwhile the members of audience in the hall who were enjoying the comedy were shouting and I couldn't converse. I went out of the hall.

I told the police operator, "Look! after retirement from police service, I have joined an organisation which runs a few hospitals and as part of my duty I am in and out of hospitals everyday". He sighed audibly and said, "Sir! please don't mistake me, one or two press reporters spoke to us sometime back saying that you are in a hospital and something has happened to you and we should check. We checked on TV also and that's why I am calling you". I playfully asked him, "Did they tell you that I am dead?". There was a long silence at the other end. He bypassed by question and said that he will ask the press reporters to speak to me directly and ended the conversation.

As I was going back home, my phone rang. The caller who identified himself as a TV reporter asked, 'Am I speaking to retired DGP?' I said yes. His next question was, 'Are you alive, sir?' I retorted saying, 'Do you think you are speaking to my ghost?' Sensing my anger he said, "Sir! one of our sources informed us that an IPS officer of 1974 or 1975 batch had expired and when I started checking, I was told that you were in the hospital and I put the two and two together". I didn't know whether to laugh or shout. I said, "Dear friend, I don't belong to both the batches you mentioned" and disconnected the call.

On reaching home, I switched on the TV. A scroll stating that I was hale and healthy started appearing.

56

Belgian Chocolates

We were visiting our son in Brussels along with my nephew Ramu, a teenager. One night during dinner my son informed us that he would take us to a chocolate factory and my nephew jumped at this suggestion. When I refused to go my wife retorted saying, ***"Sir! you may not like sweets, but we all do, Ramu is very fond of chocolates, and his mother specifically asked me to bring a box or two of the world famous Belgian Praline chocolates".*** I beat a hasty retreat when all the three insisted on doing the factory round.

The next day, we took a bus and reached the famous Neuhaus chocolate factory. Our son who met us there, led us to shop in front of the factory. He said, "Look, this is a factory outlet. You can taste any chocolate on display and decide which one to buy. If you like some particular flavour you have to buy a minimum of one kilo." Addressing my nephew he warned, "Ramu, while you are permitted to eat any chocolate, you cannot pocket anything. Even if you take one piece you have to pay for one kilo."

We all nodded our heads and trooped inside. It was a very big showroom. There were over a hundred different varieties of chocolates. There were assistants to help us know the flavour of each variety on display. The entire premises was full of chocolate aroma and we thought we were in seventh heaven.

My wife was the first to open her mouth, not for popping up a piece of chocolate, but to remark. "Hey, if we buy chocolates here it is 75% less than outside and if we buy three kilos, we get a further discount." So saying, she went ahead to purchase the flavours, she liked most.

Ramu was only interested in tasting the goodies on offer. I knew that since childhood, he had a weakness for chocolates. I watched him pop in samples of all chocolates on display. At one stage I had to stop him saying that it is bad manners to gobble so many pieces. We bought a few kilograms of chocolates and reached home fully contented.

As we were about to go to bed, Ramu complained of uneasiness and wanted to use the wash room. As he got up to walk a few steps, I noticed that his gait was unsteady and before he reached the wash room, he collapsed. My wife and son were worried and didn't know what to do. They knew getting a doctor home in Belgium was very expensive and wanted me to call our family doctor at Bengaluru and seek his advice.

I did not react to their suggestion which immensely angered them. Undeterred, I made a concoction and made Ramu swallow it and soon he became alright and went to sleep. My wife asked me what magic I had performed. I explained that many Belgium Praline chocolates are filled with spirits and Ramu had unwittingly consumed more than a chota peg of alcohol and its toxic effect was the cause of his discomfort.

On waking up the next day, Ramu resolved; he would never eat Belgian Chocolates again.

Index

Air Traffic Control, 130
  Lack of Comprehension, 130
Alcohol Detection, 35
Almora, 165
Andamans, 127
Andhra *Gongura Pachedi*, 126
Andre Malraux, 162
Anti-Corruption Bureau, 119
'Antigone' Play, 81
Anti-Sikh Sentiments, 165
Apple Watches, 152
Architectural Marvels, 162
Aristotle, 82
Arms Drill, 26
Army Mess, 165
Ashoka, 133
Assam Tea, 32, 33, 86
Assembly Elections, 119
Astu Gods, 130
Author,
  As Assistant Superintendent of Police, 20, 25
  As Police Chief of City, 40
  As Police Commissioner, 34
  Became Grandpa, 141
  Colleague Harish, 120
  Detention at Heathrow Airport, 72, 73
  First Visit to US, 73
  In Bangkok, 153

In Delhi for Civil Services Examination, 162
In Hanoi, 154
Knee Problem, 123
Learned About Non-Aligned Movement, 162
Love for HMT Watches, 151
Love for Horticulture, 54
On Deputation in Central Police Force, 65
Owner of HMT Watch—from DAD, 150
Posting to Police Station to Learn Station Work, 20
Practical Training As IPS in Karnataka District, 19
Promotion as Deputy Inspector General of Police (Police Range), 54
Promotion as Superintendent of Police, 16
Promotion as Superintendent of Police in a Communal Sensitive District, 57
Pucca Vegatarian and Addicted to Curd Rice, 126
Received Official Gift from the Foreigner, 43
Security Duties with Emir from the Gulf, 43
Selection for Training in England, 37
Served Police Department more than 3 Decades, 44
Special GPS, 156
To Kausani in Uttarakhand with Wife, 165
To School Reunion, 80
To USA, 147, 151
Tour to Srinagar, 151
Training as Circle Inspector, 60
Transit Flat in Pragati Vihar, 69
Trip to Australia, 127
Visit to
  Africa to attend International Workshop, 102
  Balaji Temple, 148
  Bengaluru Habba (Dance Festival), 81
  Disneyland Hongkong, 73
  Egypt and South Africa, 138
  Israel, 127
  Kanyakumari Alongwith his Wife, 24
  New York with Wife, 73
  Niagara Falls, 148
  Rome with Wife, 99
  Son in Brussels, 169
  Temple with Wife, 17-18
  Thailand, 73
  US, 135
Went to Receive DGP on District Border, 19
Went to See Comic Play, 167
Wife Pleased to have a Nice Labrador as a Gift, 83
With his Son in Ghent, Belgium After

Retirement, 123
Working as Staff Officer in Paramilitary Establishment in New Dehi, 31
Author's
A Canine Lover after Marriage, 105
Family Trip to Chandigarh, 14
Fiancee fond of Dogs, 83
First Posting as Asst. SP, 63
Nephew Ramu, 94
Retirement in 2011, 10
Return to City Centre to Sydney, 164
Tenure at Delhi, 90

Bachat Yojana of Government, 111
Balaji Temple, 136, 148
Bangalore
Palace, 78
Turf Club, 108
Bangkok Airport, 73
Bangladesh, 162
Bar Association, 35
Belgian
Chocolates, 169
Praline Chocolates, 169
Belgium, 154
Embassy, 162
Bhutto, Dog's Name, 133
Black Henna, 121
Brahma-Muhurta, 153
Brahmaputra, 86
Breath Analysers, 34, 35
Breeds of Pet Dogs, 154

Cape Town, 153
Cattle Station, 40
Central
Paramilitary Force, 68
Police Unit, 28
Ceremonial Uniform, 69
Chamunda Cup, 108
Chanakyapuri, 161-162
Chandragupta Maurya, 161
Chicago, 147
Chief's Office-DGA's Office, 23
Chinese Dance, 154
Chocolate Factory, 169
Chow Chow Bath, 60
Christmas Day, 95
Chutney Powder, 72, 73, 75, 126
Club Circle, 36
Colosseum, 100
Comic Interludes, 82
Common People Party (CPP), 118, 119
Congress Peanuts, 75
Course Director, 38
Cubbon Park, 89
Curd Rice, 30, 100, 127
Customs Officers, 126
Czech Republic, 162

Darjeeling Tea, 32
Day Dreaming, 79
Deccan Herald, English Newspaper, Bangalore, 10, 111
Dev Anand, 76
DGP of State, 19
Dharwad Pedas, 114
Diplomatic Enclave in Delhi, 165
District Border, 19
Dog

Handlers, 52, 53, 106
Squad, 51-53
Kamla, German Shepherd, 51
Sindhu, 51
Vimla, German Shepherd, 51
Dogs Names
As Hitler, Churchill, Khrushev and Nero, 133
On Army Ranks, 133
Dress Code, 108
Drunk Goons, 153
DTC Buses, 89
Dy. Police Commissioner, 49

Effects of Chemicals in Hair Dyes, 121
Embassies Close to Chanakyapuri, 161
Canada, 161
Finland, 161, 162
Russia, 161
Sweden, 161
US, 161, 162
Embassy,
Belgium, 162
Pakistan (Blue Domed), 162
Uzbek, 163
Exchange Mela, 112

Filipino Nationhood, 162
Finnish Embassy, 162
First Dress, Ceremonial Tunic, 23
Flemish Province, 123
Fountains, 100
Fontano Del Moro,100
Navona, 100
Trevi, 100

Gandhi, 133
General Elections, 58
Gen-Jose Artigas Road, 162
German Shepherd-named as Kempa Gowda, 133
Ghana, 154
Ghent, A Historical Town in Belgium, 123
Gojja Paste, 126
GPS Navigation, 157
Greek Tragedy, 82
Green Channel of Customs, 126
Gulf King, 44

Hampi, 100
Hanuman Chalisa, 130
Haridwar and Rishikesh, 95
Harshvardhana, 133
Heathrow Airport London, 72
HMT Watch
Factory, 151, 152
The Joy of-, 150, 151
Horse Races, 108, 109
Hotel Ashoka, 162
Hubli, 114
Bus Stand, 114
Huriyatappa, Anti-India, 92

Ilkal Sarees, 114
Immigration, 73
Indian
Chief of Protocol, 91
Dress, 78
Teachers, 147
Watches, as Good as Swiss and Japanese, 151
Wedding, 94
Injectable Polio Vaccine (IPV), 139

Inspection Campaign, 63
Inter-State Criminal, 66
ISI, 91
Israeli Security, 128
IT Firms, 149

Jackfruit-As Brahmans Mutton, 93
Joint Police Commissioner, 49
Jyotirlinga Temple, 97

Kanjeevaram, 136
Kannadigas, 132, 151
Karnataka
  Bhawan Chanakyapuri, 162
  District, 19
Kempana, Constable, 41, 42
Kendriya Vidyalaya, 69, 70
Khara Pongal and Curd Rice, 30
Kichadi with Keema, 60
KR Market Mysore, 154
Kudligi, 20
Kwame Nkruma, Ghana, 162

Lakshman, Constable, 48-50
Landmarks of Rome, 100
Language,
  Hindi, 148
  Tamil, 148
  Telugu, 147
Lentil Gosht, 91, 92
Lhasa,
  Apso Pup, A Female, 13
  Or Pomeranian, 13
London Airport, 147
Lord Balaji Idol, 135
Lost Property Room, 67
Lunch with Musharraf, 91

Madame Sheba, 93
Main Streets, 162
  Dharma Marg, 162
  Niti Marg, 162
  Nyaya Marg, 162
  Satya Marg, 162
  Vinaya Marg, 162
Mannekin Pis Monument in Brussels, 106
Menezes, Prof. 82
Mizoram, 28
MTR-Pre-Cooked Heat and Eat Food, 127
Multigatawny Soup, 91, 92
Municipal Cattle Pound, 41
Museums and Monuments, 99
Musharraf, Pervez, Gen., 91, 92
Music Classes, 136

Naseeruddin and Rathna Shah, Actors, 81
National
  Carriers, 158, 160
  Political Party (NPP), 118
Nector-Drops of Human Kindness, 164
Nehru, 133
Neuhaus Chocolate Factory, 169
Night
  Life, 153
  Shift Workers, 153
Nilgiris Tea, 32
North East, 87

Occupational Hazards, 48
Operation SOMRAS, 34
Oral Polio Vaccine (OPV), 139

Padmavati Temple, 29

Paki, Name of Pet, 133
Pakistan, 92
    And China, 133
    Embassy (Blue Domed), 162
Panchsheel Marg, 162
Panduranga Bellary,
  Constable, 26
Parliamentary
    Elections, 118, 119
    Polls, 108
Payasam, 142
    Sweet Dish made of Milk,
      143
Peace as India's Mantra, 162
Pho, Soup with Rice Noodles,
  154
Photo Shoot, 78
Plain Yoghurt, 127
Plaza Del Poppola, 100
Police
    Academy, 20
    Act, 40
    Environment, 10
    Hierarchical Set Up, 10
    Sub Culture, 10
    Terminology, 23
    Training College, 23
Pongal and Vada, 136
Pragati Vihar Campus, 69
Pranks of Chinese Puppy, 13
Property Disputes, 44
Protocol Chief, 92
Public Private Sector (PPS), 162
Puliyogari, 135, 136

Queen of Sheba, 110

Radio Operator, 20
Raising Day, 31
    Parade, 32
Ramu, Author's Nephew,
  169-171
Red Tapism, 10
Ritual Restrictions, 129
Roman Forum, 100
    Contains Oldest Structure
      of Ancient City, 100
Rome, 99
Rose Garden, 55
Rural Police Stations, 25, 26
Russian and Pakistanis, 162

Saluting Base, 52
San Matin, Argentinian
  Leader, 162
Satyanarayan Puja, 39
Security Measures post-9/11,
  127
Senior
    Bureaucrat (SB), 117
    Citizens, 124, 139
    Stewardnesss, 158-160
        Leadership Qualities,
          160
Sex Workers, 153
Shantipath, 162
Sharma, 38, 39
Shiva Temple, 16
Shiva's Vahana, 40
Sinha, Shatrugan, MP, 132
Slovakia, 162
Social Revolutions, 149
South Indian
    Customs, 94
    Delicacies, 135
    Sambher, 92
Spanish Steps, 100
Spartan State Décor, 82
Sri Lanka, 154
Sri Ram Temple, 136

State Police Chief, 52
Stray Cattle Menace, 40
Sugar Peter, SP, 20
Superintendent of Police,
  Called 'Seara Papa' in Police
  Academy, 20
Suresh, 109, 110
Susan Or Steffi (Dog's name),
  13
Sushma, Ramu's Colleague, 94
Suzie, Dog's Name, 14
Suzy Or Susheela, Dog's
  Name, 14, 15
Suzy Wong, Dog's Name, 14
Swadeshi Goods, 151
Swaminarayana Temple, 136

Teas of Assam, 86
Tel Avive, 128
Temple of Goddess Durga, 57
Tibet In China, 13
Tibetan Dog, 13
Timanna, ASI, 36
Tippu Sultan, 133
Tirupati, 135
    Temple, 148
Town Police Station, 26, 40
Traditional North Indian
  Wedding, 94
Tragedies, 81
Training Batchmates of Author
  in England, 38
    Bose, 38
    Inderjit, 38
    Indu, 38
    Kashyap, 38
    Muttoo, 38
    Nambi, 38
    Srivastava, 38
Training Institute in UK, 38
Trenella, 110

UK Customs, 73
Undress, Means in Civilian
  Dress, 24
Uruguayan Nationhood, 162
US Embassy, 162
Uzbek Embassy, 163
Uzbekistan, 162

Vaccination, Vagaries of-, 138
Vanishing Trick, 54-56
Vedas, Shastras, 39
Vidhana Soudha, 23
Vidyarthi Bhavan, 136
Vohra, DGP, 23

Western Africa, Prone to
  Infection, 138
Wireless Operator, 19, 21

Yellow Fever, 138, 140
    Vaccine, 139
Yoga, 154
Yoghurt Tubs, 128